Take Back Your Mind

Buddhist Advice for Anxious Times

Lodro Rinzler

AUTHOR OF *SIT LIKE A BUDDHA*

Cover and text design by Jess Morphew

Cover art by Malte Mueller/ Getty Images

ISBN: 9781735150109

Library of Congress Control Number: 2020922671

1 2 3 4 5 / 24 23 22 21 20

Take Back
Your Mind

To Adreanna. I am lucky for your love.

Contents

PART TWO

The Good News: You Can Relax

PART THREE

From Anxiety to Compassionate Activity

PART FOUR

Rubber, Meet Road: The Practical Application for Your Anxious Lifestyle

Introduction

Let's talk about why you're anxious all the time. If I asked you about your stress-level, you might tell me it's high and that's because:

» Work is overwhelming.
» There are endless money woes.
» Your partner broke up with you.
» Family issues are coming to a head.
» The world is breaking your goddamn heart.

Here's the thing though: those are the stories going on with you—right now. Tomorrow, you may get promoted at work, making the time and money issues seem less daunting, or you may begin to date someone new and find real joy in their company, or your family may sit down and hash things out. The world does tend to feel like it's on fire most days, but maybe your anxiety drops its focus on the world's issues and moves on to something else. All of a sudden, the situation that caused you so much pain evaporates from your mind and you forget why you were so stuck on it to begin with. That's what anxiety does: it looks for ways to take over your mind and sap your mental energy until you feel fucking awful—and then anxiety moves on to something new to focus on to repeat the same cycle.

I know because I've suffered with anxiety all my life. Ten-year-old me couldn't attend a sleepover at a friend's house because it was too stressful. Even though I started meditating at age six, it's not like I was able to breathe away all the stressful triggers from my life (nor will I expect you to). I've had to work with multiple modalities, including various meditation techniques offered in this book and ways of discerning how to reduce certain triggers, and look at anxiety itself to live a life that allows me to notice when anxiety arises, acknowledge it, and come back to reality.

I will say that meditation has helped me *with* stress as opposed to my life being "stress-free" because I don't think such an existence is possible. Having taught Buddhist meditation for the last nineteen years, I have seen any number of stressful occasions arise in my own and my meditation students' lives. No one has figured out how to completely eradicate stress. That's the bad news. The good news is that we can learn to notice when anxiety arises and not go down the rabbit hole all the time. Instead of focusing our attention on the story of the day—be it based in your work, money, relationships, family, or society—we can focus our attention on the anxiety itself. We can look anxiety dead in the eyes and say, "Actually, I prefer to spend my mental energy elsewhere thank you." From there, we can allow anxiety to move through us, allowing us to rest into a sense of relaxation that is always waiting to be discovered.

The lessons presented in this book stem from the Buddhist tradition but are made for everyone. I've aimed to make the teachings accessible in a way that you can employ both the formal Buddhist meditation practices and on-the-spot techniques that can

Believe it or not, you're not inherently anxious. You're inherently whole, good, and kind as is. When we rest in meditation, we discover that underneath the stories we tell ourselves about our anxiety is anxiety itself. When we look at anxiety itself, we realize it's a hell of a lot more ephemeral than we might have suspected. In fact, underneath the anxiety is innate peace.

What you hold is a guidebook to working with your mind so that anxiety doesn't rule your life. On a deeper level, it is a practical toolbox you can draw from so you come to embody mindfulness and compassion. On a deeper level, it's about realizing your own basic goodness, developing trust in that experience, and seeing it in others so that we realize the goodness in society overall. Thank you for joining me on this path. Let's work together to take back your mind.

Lodro Rinzler
June 1, 2020

take back your mind—without having to subscribe to an trappings or ideology.

That said, the book does revolve around the thi or "vehicles" that the Buddha taught twenty-six hund ago. The first is the foundational vehicle, sometimes re as the Hinayana. I don't love that phrase, as the trans the term *hina* can denote this is a "narrow" or "lesser" you'll notice I'll be referring to it as "foundational." Foun implies that the first step in our journey to take back the m look directly at the ways we perpetuate our own sufferin minimize the harm we cause ourselves and others. Founc also points to one fundamental aspect we can draw from: o basic goodness (more on that shortly).

Once we have that foundational base established in S I, by opening our hearts and minds to others, we can wid focus beyond our anxiety. Sections II and III focus on w known as the Mahayana path. *Maha* can be translated as "gr and *yana* as "vehicle." This path is a way that allows us to li life from a place of compassion, balanced with an understa of reality as it is.

We build on the as-it-is-ness in Section IV as we touc the Vajrayana teachings, another path within Buddhism. *Vaj* "indestructible" while *yana* remains "vehicle." (I swear this b is not littered with a lot of foreign terms but these are impor so I'm getting them out there up-front.) The indestructible asp of who we are is our innate wakefulness. We can live our viewing it not as some challenge we need to get through but inherently sacred, should we choose to show up authentically a wholeheartedly for it.

CHAPTER 1

Why Am I Stressed the F*ck Out?

Recently, I was at dinner with friends. The music was pleasant enough, the food tasty, and the company divine. It's rare this particular group gathers together so it felt like a real treat. At some point, the topic of politics came up (as it tends to at times), and I noticed when my friend Jonathan changed the subject. Later on, while we were exiting the restaurant, I took him aside and asked how he was doing. "I'm sorry about earlier," he said, "but I've gotten so anxious, I have to watch a half hour of animal videos each night just to come back to some semblance of normal."

I had no idea my friend's anxiety had risen to this level, and while I was saddened to hear it, I figured watching animals play was better than what so many of us do to lessen the overwhelm that plagues us. Some are so on edge, they habitually pick up a bottle and pour a drink. Others prefer popping pills. Some throw themselves into work in some hopeless effort to "catch up" and be free of work anxiety, pretending that tomorrow won't bring new emails to respond to. So . . . animal videos? I could shrug and accept my friend's coping mechanism pretty easily.

PART ONE

Let's Talk About Why You're Anxious All The Time

The conversation stuck with me, giving birth to my noticing how all-pervasive and perpetual anxiety is for so many people. It's not just my friend who was experiencing new levels of stress leading to anxiety. According to one study, anxiety is the number one mental health problem among women and is second only to alcohol and drug abuse among men. Yet, this rampant problem is rarely addressed as a public health epidemic. Close to forty million people in the United States suffer from an anxiety disorder, according to the Anxiety and Depression Association of America.[1]

If we're honest (and I'd like to think we can be with one another), that's exactly what it is—an epidemic. Anxiety is the monkey so many of us carry on our backs, one we always want to be rid of, yet rarely discuss.

I just used two terms and should probably define them: stress and anxiety. Stress is considered to be your body's reaction to a trigger—be it an angry email in your inbox or heavy traffic—and is generally a short-term experience. Anxiety, on the other hand, has been defined as a "sustained mental health disorder" which may arise from a stressful trigger but doesn't fade away.[2] Anxiety has both a cognitive element and a physiological response (in the form of stress), which means we experience anxiety in both our mind and our body.

One way to think about the distinction between stress and anxiety is that stress is a response to a threat while anxiety manifests even when there is no clear and present danger. Your rent is due and you don't have the funds to pay it? Here, we are talking about a stress trigger. Obsessing about an awkward conversation with your landlord? You've moved into anxiety, focusing not on a true danger but a spiraling pattern now holding you in a fight-or-flight response. In other words, anxiety gets lodged in the mind and sticks around for the long haul leading to: frequent headaches, restless sleep, feeling light-headed, faint, or dizzy, frequent illness, irritability, gastrointestinal problems, feeling overwhelmed, poor concentration, forgetfulness, and even loss of sexual desire.[3] Anxiety is like a hidden veil that keeps us cut off from the world around us. Like an actual veil, it obscures our vision—we are unable to see beyond the thing stressing us out today.

But what if I told you that you could lift the veil? That once you do so, there is a big, beautiful world you can enjoy just because, quite simply, you are seeing beyond your layer of stress and anxiety?

Here is where I tell you about meditation. Granted, I'm a meditation teacher and have been guiding people in the practice for more than half my life; I started teaching at the age of eighteen while I was still in college. I was raised by Buddhist parents and started meditating when I was six years old. When I was a kid, it was considered weird; it wasn't the only reason I was pushed into lockers in high school, but the fact that I meditated didn't help. Now the practice has become so ubiquitous, I'd be willing to bet ten dollars the same kid who pushed me into a locker is now pressing play on some guided meditation app.

And why not? These days, when you skim social media, you will find a new scientific study coming out each week listing the benefits of a consistent meditation practice. You sleep better.[4] You boost your immune system.[5] You're more productive. You're more creative. And your Tinder matches go through the roof.

To be clear, I'm making the last example up. Or, rather, the improved ability to get dates as a result of meditation had not yet been scientifically proven when I wrote this book. But the rest of these benefits are real. A shrewd reader may even notice I left out one well-known benefit: stress reduction.

The reason I didn't lead with stress reduction is twofold. First, take another look at that list. Those benefits strike me as ancillary aspects of you being less stressed-out. If you had less stress, you'd sleep better right? You'd be more productive at work because, well, you're focused on the project at hand since you're not trapped by anxiety. If your body isn't being held in a fight-or-flight response mode, yeah, I'm guessing it would heal better and you'd have more room for creativity. These benefits come with you simply being less stressed-out.

The second reason I didn't lead with stress reduction is because I think the term is a bit of a misnomer. If you develop a meditation practice, it unfortunately doesn't mean you get to have a better life than everyone else and less stressful things happen to you. You still have whatever money problems exist for you right now, whether you meditate or not. Your ex is still your ex. Your annoying family member still pesters you regularly. The stressors are still there, not somehow reduced in size à la *Honey I Shrunk the Kids*.

On the surface "stress reduction" makes it sound like if you meditate you won't have stressful things ever happen to you. Your email inbox will be empty of people asking you to do things, your loved ones will act exactly what you hope they will, and every time you flick on the television the world will be showcasing sheer perfection. Yet that's simply not the world we live in.

Here's the good news: meditation *will* change the way you relate to those things. You may realize your credit card bill is due, but you are more trained to take a breath and enjoy your morning coffee, as opposed to spending every minute between now and then stressing yourself out about it. Your ex is still your ex, but thanks to meditation they are taking up less mental real estate then they used to. Your annoying family member still does their annoying thing, but you don't carry it with you throughout your day; you are more able to acknowledge what they did and put it down.

I have meditated for over thirty years and can say pretty definitively I still have anxiety-producing scenarios in my life. Unfortunately, we can't take something like meditation and say it will magically erase the potential for stressful situations. Instead, we need to shift our thinking about meditation so our common definition is based in developing a different relationship with stress.

If the world is figuratively and sometimes quite literally going to continue to be on fire (I'm looking at you, California and Australia), we need multiple tools to remain grounded, sane and yes, even open-hearted, in these troubling times. Watching animal videos is a wonderful thing to do, but we're only treating the symptoms of anxiety. At some point, we need to roll up our sleeves and treat the disease.

You can live without so much anxiety and stress. You can train the mind to find contentment, peace and joy—even in the midst of difficult circumstances. It takes a bit of work, but the benefits last a lifetime.

CHAPTER 2

The Three Realms of Anxious Thought

All experience is preceded by mind,
Led by mind,
Made by mind.
Speak of act with a peaceful mind,
And happiness follows
Like a never-departing shadow.

—The Buddha[6]

There are a zillion other translations of the words above from the Buddha, including the ubiquitous "We are what we think," which means that whatever begins in our thoughts manifests in a myriad of ways in our lives. Every experience we have originates with what arises in the mind, so we need to understand how our minds work.

To better understand the mind, let's talk about three realms we are always playing in: the individual, the interpersonal, and the societal.

In the individual realm, here you are with your own mind, which is sometimes wild and stressed-out, and you have to give it space to settle in order to properly address your anxiety. In the interpersonal realm, when you get up off the meditation seat, you encounter people you like, people you dislike, and individuals you don't know. They too are anxious and suffering and if you're not careful, you bring your suffering into conversation with their suffering and everyone suffers worse. In the societal realm, society is a fancy term for the people mentioned above. It is not some big thing *out there*—it's here, right now, made up of you and those people you like, dislike, and ignore.

When you are riding the train for the morning commute, your train car is a temporary society you are participating in. You can choose to show up and engage it in a kind way, smiling at your neighbors and offering your seat when needed. Alternatively, you can sit and hide from everyone, or act out on any stress and frustration due to delays and negatively affect the people around you. It's your choice! And you are constantly offered it.

In addition to the commuting society, there is your work society, your family society, and even your home society of you and a roommate or romantic partner or cat. These are each societies we are cocreating in any given moment. How you show up for these societies is entirely within your control, and the path to positively affecting them is based in working with your own mind. The more you understand your own mind, the more you see how your thoughts ultimately affect your speech and activity, thus affecting those people you like, dislike and often don't even notice, and how we come together to make up this thing we call a society.

Imagine putting on rose-colored glasses. Whatever you looked at during your day would appear pink, right? This is the way anxiety works on us. Once we've connected fully to anxiety and let it color our experience, we view the world through our current anxiety-ridden storyline. We see something in the news and think, "Will this be a good thing for me? Or will it only make the thing I'm stressed about worse?" We hit traffic on our way to work and we think, "I'll be late for work for a second time this month—they might fire me!" When the cars begin moving again, we let that thought go and find another external factor to reinforce our negative storyline.

We view our personal life, our interpersonal relationships, and everyone around us through the lens of anxiety. The teachings and meditation practices offered in this book allow us to take those rose-colored glasses off so we can begin to see reality more clearly.

CHAPTER 3

Calm-Abiding Meditation

If you can accept your body, then you have a chance to see your body as your home. You can rest in your body, settle in, relax, and feel joy and ease . . . You have to accept yourself as you are.

—Thich Nhat Hanh, *How to Love*[7]

I am going to ask you to do something scary: be with your mind. The way we will do that is through meditation.

Have I sold you on this meditation thing yet? Good Lord, I hope so. This is my seventh book on the topic and while I'm tickled these things continue to be picked up and read by good humans such as yourself, I do know for a fact if someone doesn't actually start to do the practice while reading these words, then they won't really see the transformation I promise.

This particular transformation is part of the foundational path of Buddhism. When I was growing up in a Buddhist household, this path was often referred to as the *Hinayana*, which can be translated as "narrow vehicle." I find that term a bit derogatory, and as mentioned in the introduction, I prefer "foundational," as there is nothing narrow about working with your own mind and heart to ultimately help other people. The teachings in this first section of the book fall under the foundational vehicle, including my favorite practice to introduce: *shamatha*.

Shamatha is a Sanskrit word which can be translated as "calm-abiding" or "peaceful abiding." You may have heard it referred to as "mindfulness of the breath." Mindfulness is best described as being with what is occurring in the present moment, without judgment. Anxiety, meanwhile, is being with what could maybe, possibly, be and judging that possibility as negative. Shamatha, as a practice, is a way for us to make peace with ourselves and our world, even if it doesn't always look peaceful out there. It is not a way to change our external circumstances and eliminate stressful situations entirely (if you can find the magic wand that can, please let me know). Instead, we take a long hard look at stress and come to the remarkable conclusion that we don't have to chase every anxiety-producing thought popping up.

Here's my caveat: shamatha is hard. It's worth it, but like learning any new skill, it takes some practice and getting used to. The short instructions are as follows:

>» Take an upright yet relaxed posture.
>» Feel your body breathing.
>» When you get distracted, return your attention to your breath.

That's it. You might think, "Wow, it's so simple, even I can do it!" You plop yourself down, imagining you will sit there in peace for a while before a thought comes along, only to discover your mind is scattered and you have thousands of thoughts within the first minute. At this juncture, saying we can tame the anxious mind in meditation is akin to wading into the ocean and trying to turn the tide back with your two hands.

If you start at the place where your mind feels incredibly busy, cool. Really. This is the flavor of your mind on a given day. Perhaps the next day it gets a bit easier to find and stay with the breath. A week of consistent practice later and you're hanging out with the breath for a few cycles of it flowing in and out before you get distracted. What was initially hard now seems a bit more straightforward.

In the same way you may have trained in other areas of your life (learning a musical instrument or working your way toward running a marathon, for example), here you start where you are and build out your learning incrementally over time. Not unlike going from awkwardly gripping the guitar to playing songs by *The Cure* or sweating after a short jog to running twenty-plus miles, here you're going from a super stressed-out mind to one more willing to relax—even in stressful situations.

Detailed Shamatha Instruction

The simplest way to describe shamatha (peaceful abiding meditation) is when we relax with the natural sensation of the breath and, when we inevitably get distracted, we return to this stabilizing influence over and over again.* To break it out a bit, here are the three elements to consider: body, breath, and mind.

---

* You can find a recording of this meditation at lodrorinzler.com/anxiety.

BODY

» Take a relaxed yet uplifted posture. Feel the weight of your body sink into the cushion or chair beneath you. If you are sitting on the ground, loosely cross your legs so that the knees fall a little bit below your hips. If you prefer to kneel, that is fine. Just keep your legs parallel to not add strain on your back. It's important that you feel grounded when you sit down to meditate.

» Gently lift up through your spine, almost like there is a string at the top of your head pulling you toward the sky.

» Allow the muscles in your shoulders and back to relax around this strong skeletal structure.

» Pick your hands up at the elbows and drop the palms down on your thighs—this is a natural axis point on the body, allowing for support for your back.

» Let your skull balance naturally at the top of the spine with your chin slightly tucked in.

» Relax the muscles in your face and gently unclench the jaw. You can even place your tongue against the roof of your mouth to allow for clear breathing.

» If you are accustomed to meditating with your eyes closed, no problem. Let your lids gently shut. Since we are attempting to wake up to what is happening in the present moment, I recommend you try meditating with your eyes open, with your gaze resting three to five feet ahead of you on the ground in a relaxed and loose manner.

BREATH

There are so many areas of our life where we are tempted to fix, control, or manipulate whatever is happening. In shamatha practice, we let go of those anxiety-producing tendencies and relax with the physical sensation of the breath, as it is.

» As you breathe in, notice you're breathing in.
» As you breathe out, relax with the sensation of breathing out.
» Nothing to fix, nothing to change. Just relax with the breath.

MIND

» Some meditation teachers claim that we experience 60,000 to 80,000 thoughts a day. I would argue that at times, it feels like all of those thoughts come rushing in all at once the moment you sit down to meditate. You will have thoughts; it is completely normal. Getting rid of thoughts is not the point—that is simply impossible to do. Asking the mind to stop thinking is akin to asking the heart to stop beating. Instead, we acknowledge when a thought tries to take us away from the present moment. We acknowledge it and return to the soothing and stabilizing influence of the breath.

» If it is helpful, you can say "thinking" when you notice you have drifted off into the past or the future. You see that there are thoughts, you acknowledge them with "thinking," and then you return to feeling the body breathing. We do so over and over again.

» It is important that we treat ourselves with tremendous friendliness during meditation. If you are experiencing a lot of thoughts, you may be tempted (after playing out the same argument in your head for the twelfth time) to go from saying "thinking" to internally yelling at yourself, "THINKING!" Here you are perpetuating the aggression that has arisen, instead of seeing it for what it is and choosing to not give into it.

» When you notice yourself getting frustrated, try to say "thinking" to yourself in the kindest tone, almost like you're trying to coax a puppy out from under a bed during a thunderstorm. The puppy is there, freaked out, and we soften our heart and say, "Come on buddy, let's do this together."

A Variation on the Traditional Technique

Although I was trained in shamatha to use the word "thinking," I have found in our modern age, because so many of us perpetuate self-aggression during our meditation, it might be helpful to take this idea to another level to counter such a tendency. Instead of saying "thinking" when you drift off, you could instead use the words "I love you." It is somewhat harder to get super-aggressive with yourself when you are offering forgiveness and acceptance by saying "I love you."

Please note: saying "I love you" is not the traditional Buddhist thing to do and while I rarely stray from the traditional teachings, this is an experiment I am inviting you into. If you want to join me in this experiment, choose a meditation session to try saying these three words when you find yourself distracted: "I love you." Here, you are offering yourself a moment of kindness before coming back to the body breathing. Don't switch between "thinking" and "I love you" in one practice period. You will end up being distracting and will spend the whole session attempting to judge which one you prefer. You can try both on different days and see which resonates for you.

Regardless of what you say to yourself when you drift off in meditation, the main point is that you can be gentle with yourself each time you return to the breath. You can offer yourself warm acceptance and understanding while simultaneously interrupting the stressful thoughts when they arise. Each time you acknowledge you have drifted off and return to the breath, you are creating new neural pathways based on the following belief: "I don't have to chase after every anxious thought that comes up." This realization is extremely good news and through it we come to understand that the practice is extremely good for us. The more we can befriend the totality of who we are in meditation, the less of a grip anxiety has on us.

Shamatha—or mindfulness of the breath practice—is the foundation of every other practice I will introduce in this book. By taking the time to be with the body breathing, we learn more about who we truly are. We learn that we don't have to chase those anxious stories that pop up, we can relax and come to accept ourselves, and we don't have to build a cocoon in order to hide from the world around us.

CHAPTER 4

Slicing through the Cocoon

We surround ourselves with our own familiar thoughts, so that nothing sharp or painful can touch us. We are so afraid of our own fear that we deaden our hearts.

—Chögyam Trungpa Rinpoche,
Shambhala: Sacred Path of the Warrior[8]

Many of us walk around with a suit of armor on, made up of our own anxiety and neurosis. In the Shambhala tradition, the lineage of Buddhism I was initially trained in, there is a great term for this armor: *cocoon*. We are so lost in our own heads that we spin story after story about whatever is stressing us out that day, covering ourselves in a thick layer of thoughts only about ourselves such that it's hard to see beyond this cocoon of our own creation.

The more we focus on "me" and "what I need," the thicker the cocoon becomes and the less we pay attention to the world around us. We do this consistently in the hopes that nothing painful or fear-inducing can get to us. It may even take someone texting us out of the blue and calling our attention to a personal crisis or getting (yet another) alert on our phone saying a national tragedy has occurred for us to snap out of the anxiety-du-jour and open our hearts to others.

When you meditate regularly though, it *does* something to this cocoon. It takes a tiny knife to its layers, gradually slicing through these threads of our neurosis. Each time you notice the anxious thoughts and return to the breath, you're cutting through the tendency to spin out entirely and the walls of the cocoon soften.

People are very much interested in the idea of mindfulness and being more present, but once you've done the practice for a while you start to understand that it also makes you very kind. Shamatha allows you a chance not just to get to know yourself better or see your stress more clearly. Every time you get lost in thought and come back, shamatha is actually an opportunity for you to be kind to yourself. "Oh, I drifted off again—okay, not a big deal, back to the breath."

This is the opposite of what many of us do, which is use meditation as a way to beat ourselves up further: "I am such a jerk!" "I can barely stay with the breath." "I'm failing at life, including my meditation." Yikes. That amount of self-aggression is a lot to put on yourself. As I mentioned in the shamatha instruction, the best thing to do is treat yourself with unconditional friendliness whenever you drift off, planting seeds of kindness alongside the seeds of being more present.

When you have established a deep meditation practice, it's like picking up a jackhammer, placing it right at the center of the cocoon, and turning the thing on to full strength. The more you meditate, the more you cut through the layers of confusion around your heart, leaving you in a very vulnerable, raw, and loving state. The act of meditation is an act of fearlessness. In the Shambhala tradition, fearlessness does not mean finding some secret dimension where we no longer experience fear. It means you look directly at fear and stay present with it until it shifts and changes.

When fearful or anxiety-producing thoughts come up in meditation, you have a choice: you can chase after them or you can try something new. You can try to let go of the stories you tell yourself and simply be with the emotion underneath. You are training to feel what you feel without judgment.

When you are able to sit with your current experience, whether it is good, bad, or ugly, you notice the cocoon begins to become less rigid; you can poke your head out of it and breathe once more. You become more available to the world around you and can enjoy your daily experiences. Water tastes delicious. The sun's warmth is healing. The excited bark of the dog warms your heart. These things were already present before, but it took you looking directly at your mind and relaxing your hold on yourself to begin to notice them. In fact, you may even start to glimpse that you can let go of your tight layers of habitual patterns and anxiety entirely, loosening your ego enough to glimpse your basic goodness.

CHAPTER 5

Who is it That's Suffering from Anxiety?

We're all born naked and the rest is drag.

—RuPaul Charles, *Lettin it All Hang Out: An Autobiography*

RuPaul Charles has revolutionized drag culture and has made it accessible like no one else. He has a number of catchphrases he is fond of repeating including "We're all born naked and the rest is drag," which is perhaps the most accurate depiction of the Buddhist notion of samsara I have ever heard. *Samsara* is a Sanskrit term which denotes the cycle of suffering we perpetuate in every single moment of our lives. It is how we constantly wrap ourselves in a cocoon made up of our passion, aggression, and ignorance, chasing after pleasure, and desperately trying to avoid pain. This tension between only wanting the good things in life and desperately fearing anything going wrong is where anxiety lives.

We are indeed born naked, free from anxiety and stress, but over time we are influenced by not-so-helpful stories offered up by our parents, our friends, our school teachers, celebrities—just about everyone. The stories may be:

» People who have my skin color are good people.
» People who do not have my skin color are scary or unsafe people.
» You are this gender and that is what you are meant to be forever.
» This form of sexuality is a positive way to manifest love.
» This other form of sexuality is taboo.

And so on. . . . Before we are truly able to think for ourselves, we are infused with all sorts of narratives that inform our world view. Building on RuPaul's "born naked" idea, the Zen teacher Reverend angel Kyodo williams Sensei introduced a Buddhist perspective on these narratives:

> I came gorgeous, and genius, and magic, and perfect, and aware, and compassionate, and wanting to love people, and wanting to be connected. And by a series of unfortunate events, societal structures hindered my love, and my compassion, and my desire to be connected to you, and to see you. . . . So I'm literally being liberated from, not liberating into something. I don't have to develop anything. I have to just cultivate the natural, basic goodness of my humanity that I arrived here with . . . [9]

To unpack angel's remarks, we are all born good and open, and then through societal stories taught to us by everyone (from our caregivers to the people who design Internet ads), we get bogged down with concepts that keep us from connecting fully with others. We accumulate stories that inform how we behave and who we think we ought to become. Then, we perform these narratives we've developed throughout our lives, dressing ourselves in drag with these concepts. Sharon Salzberg, cofounder of the Insight Meditation Society, once said, "We mark off the territory of our identifications, both personal and group, as though they had intrinsic meaning, whereas it is only like drawing lines in space."[10]

News flash: you are not these constructs! When you strip off the fixed ideas and expectations you have accumulated over a lifetime, you may discover limitlessness and goodness once more. You are innately peace. You are whole and complete. But you dress yourself in a lot of made-up ideas and those ideas cut you off from your experience of the present moment.

Day by day, we develop any number of opinions about what is right and wrong, whether we want to identify with some people, religions, movements, and so on. We build what Buddhists refer to as an ego out of these concepts, stacking them together Transformer-style to make one big concept to form an anxious "me." The Buddhist notion of *anātman*, which is a Sanskrit term for saying "not-self," points to the simple truth that the stories we tell ourselves to form this ego are not as permanent and real as we might suspect.

My version of "me" has so many markers I have to look at, a good number of which cause suffering:

» I am a somewhat articulate meditation teacher.
» I am a prolific author.
» I am a great husband.

» I am a kind friend.

» I have all my hair.

I could go on and on. None of these markers for who I think I am are so bad, right? But let's face it: I could give a really bad Buddhist talk tomorrow and my concept of being a decent teacher might crumble. My wife seems to like me well enough, but would she really say I'm a "great husband" every day of the year? (Likely not.) Also, my hair is definitely thinning, and I probably should not have included that on the list.

The point is that I might cling to these identifying characteristics for who I think I am, and when evidence inevitably arises to show me they are not 100% accurate, I could end up devastated and confused about what a Lodro even is anyway. Furthermore, the mental energy I expend worrying about my hair falling out or how good any given talk is going to be is wasted energy.

This is how ego works: every time something doesn't go the way I think or want it to go, in my career, love life, with friends and more, my mind registers it as an attack on my very being. This is why so many of us take a breakup not as a sign that we haven't found the right person for us but that we're inherently unworthy of love; we make it about the core of who we are, not what happened to us. We are constantly reifying and trying to prop up the ego, which perpetuates so much suffering in our own heads. It's a really hard struggle to try and make everything fall in line with the way we want it to. And it's not just you and me—literally everyone follows this pattern, which is why there is so much (self-inflicted) pain in our world.

You know the politician you think is horrible? They are a

construct of multiple layers of concept and experience informing how they act, what morals they value, and how they think the country should look. Those white supremacists marching against anyone who does not look like them? Same thing—they have (likely from a young age) been acculturated into a certain belief system that makes them think they are doing the right thing. You and I may take one look at them and call them monsters, but they believe they are heroes based on the stories they have long been told (and continue to tell themselves).

So many of the systemic issues we face right now were born long before we were, but the perpetuation of them is rooted in our own ego. As the Zen teacher Zenju Earthlyn Manuel wrote, "Race, sexuality, and gender are born out of an awareness that 'I am this.' The feelings and perceptions that follow this awareness give rise to an experience of life as appearance-based. Race, sexuality, and gender are perpetuated when past experiences of them carries forward into the present."[11] Even if we inherited concepts of race, gender, and sexuality from our parents and their parents before them, we have an opportunity—today—to confront these aspects of our ego and make more conscious choices about how we treat others.

With ego, we build a full identity over time and act from the perspective of self-preservation. However, through meditation, we can learn to undo some of these patterns and not take ourselves (or others) so seriously. We can, as RuPaul has also said, "Wear our identity like a loose garment." We can learn to question some of our assumed beliefs about who other people are and become spacious enough to accommodate different perspectives from our own, without perpetuating more suffering.

Imagine you're going about your day and someone you work

with sends you an obnoxious email. Your stories in response may include "This person is always like this. They must have been raised with no manners," or "Of course they are trying to make me look bad here—everyone is out for my position," or "If this job doesn't work out, I will be destitute, living in a box on the street."

Each day, I meet with a number of meditation students one-on-one and somehow, once there is a perceived threat at work, it gets blown up in their heads to the point where they believe they will end up destitute. This is quite the leap from one obnoxious email in an inbox. It takes some time and gentle poking to get them to realize that living in a box on the street is not the reality of the situation. The reality is someone did something other than what you wanted them to do, and this led to a "me" versus "you" mentality, triggering deep fear and anxiety.

The dualistic "me" versus "you" mentality is the basis of interpersonal suffering as well as societal suffering overall. It's how all is fine and good with a friend, until they do something you disagree with and you villainize them until things are resolved. It's when those people in government are horrible, and your party is the one actually looking out for the country. We create this polarity constantly, lumping people into the camps of who we like and dislike, based on our own expectations and decades (sometimes centuries) of belief patterns and habitual tendencies.

In the past, in my books, I would casually refer to a time when I worked on the 2012 Obama campaign as a field organizer. People would go out of their way to leave a review on Amazon: "Great book, but I wish he left his politics out of it." I cannot ignore that I have a particular lens through which I view the political world, but I can assure you, Dear Reader, I am not interested in any partisanship. The realm of politics at times appears no different than baseball; people pick a team and they want their team to win. The other team is considered garbage and we only wish the worst for them because they are evil. I am here to call bullshit.

In order for us to move toward a more sane and more compassionate society, we need to stop blaming some amorphous "other" out there for our problems. As the Tibetan Buddhist teacher Chögyam Trungpa Rinpoche once wrote, "We could blame the organization; we could blame the government; we could blame the police force; we could blame the weather; we could blame the food; we could blame the highways; we could blame our own motorcars, our own clothes; we could blame an infinite variety of things. But it is we who are not letting go, not developing enough warmth and sympathy—which makes us problematic. So we cannot blame anybody."[12]

We need to look within and address our own egoic manifestations of suffering and the ways we trap ourselves in anxiety. The more we uncover our innate peace and unearth the bias that holds us back from openly connecting with others the better. Then we can move our practice off the meditation seat and into the rest of our life, connecting with people not from a "me versus you" mentality but from the perspective of "we're in this together."

The Dalai Lama put it best when he said, "First, one must change. I first watch myself, check myself, then expect change from others."[13] The good news about how to shift our incredibly aggressive and chaotic society is simple: it starts with us getting to know ourselves better. Thus far, we have looked at our anxious thoughts, how they play out in the personal, interpersonal and societal realms, and how they can become solidified into one massive cocoon cutting us off from the world around us. We have talked about how our cocoons give birth to the solid, substantial, not-so-fun identity we so desperately cling to. Yet, through the meditation techniques—shamatha and more I'll share in this book—we can undo this chaotic ball of yarn we call an ego. In fact, there's a set of teachings I'd like to introduce you to now that can help us drop the ways we perpetuate our suffering and move to a place of greater connection.

CHAPTER 6

Social Media and the Danger of Comparing Mind

Comparison is the thief of joy.

—Attributed to Theodore Roosevelt

There's a traditional analogy in Buddhism: a man is walking in the forest when, out of nowhere, he is shot with an arrow. Now, instead of pulling it out and tending to his own healing process, he begins to spin out, thinking "Who shot me? Why am I always the one being shot? Everyone else gets to go around being happy, but I take one walk in the woods and as usual, I end up in trouble. Chuck at work deserves to be shot, not me." And so on. This mental spiraling is known as the second arrow.

Arrow #1: The suffering inflicted upon us as part of life.
Arrow #2: The suffering we inflict on ourselves in response.

One of the ways we lock ourselves in stress and anxiety is by clinging to the idea that other people have it made and we begin perpetuating lots of stories about their lives. These days, there is no better forum to indulge this idea than on social media. You can open up Instagram and, within thirty seconds of scrolling, see people who are presenting the idea that they have their act together which, of course, only perpetuates the notion that you're the only one who doesn't. In your bones, you know everyone is suffering. We all experience arrows in our lives. Most of us perpetuate the second arrow too. Yet, social media portrays the opposite, leading to us feeling isolated and alone.

I'm not saying the only way out of stress and anxiety is to delete your Facebook account (although it may not hurt). I'm saying we need to reconsider what it means to engage in these platforms from a place of self-care and responsibility.

The main route to responsible social media usage is the same one for many activities we engage in: we look at why we're doing the thing in the first place. Before we open up Facebook, we can contemplate our intention: "Why am I opening up this tab? Is it because I'm bored with work and looking to escape the feeling of boredom? Or did I want to check in on my friend, because they have been MIA lately and I want to see if they've posted?" The former might lead us to endlessly scrolling, then freaking out when we have wasted a half hour. The latter would take two minutes and lead to more skillful action.

Having grokked our intention, we can move into skillful activity. The Buddha outlined a number of guidelines for how we can communicate. In his teachings known as The Vaca Sutta, he said that any statement promotes positive communication if it meets these criteria: "It is spoken at the right time. It is spoken in truth. It is spoken affectionately. It is spoken beneficially. It is spoken with a mind of good-will."[14]

Let's break this set of teachings out and map it for something he likely could not have predicted: the tremendous influence of social media.

In regard to goodwill, we can look at our intention behind posting on social media. If we have something cool going on, is our motivation to share the good news as a result of a longing to genuinely connect and get people involved in our life? Or is it so everyone thinks we also have our act together and are doing as well as or better than they are? If we are posting with a mind of goodwill, meaning the intention is to connect and benefit everyone concerned, then that's a sign we may want to go ahead and do it. If we are going to be perpetuating the trope of someone who always has everything figured out, then we may want to contemplate whether that's worth sharing.

The next factor we can consider when posting is whether what we are sharing is beneficial and affectionate to others. Beneficial is a subjective term, but it's based in the idea that what we are sharing is meant to uplift or educate others, as opposed to tearing them down. Particularly these days, a platform like Facebook seems to be a venue for people to post a lot of political ideology, not so much with the intent of sparking genuine dialogue but to prove that their closely held views are right, daring people who disagree to argue with them.

When we see this sort of rhetoric, it may be a good idea to avoid the bait. There is an old adage that it is better to be kind than to be correct. When we are engaging with our community on social media, this simple notion can guide our hand in a way that we build bridges with people we may disagree with, as opposed to burning them and causing us further stress and grief.

Now we can move to whether what we are sharing is truthful. These days, people seem to post a lot of the glorious moments in their career or love life without acknowledging the heartache within each of us. Those who share only the seemingly endless good news of their life, with no moments of reflection, are contributing to what some call "success theater."

Success theater is when we perform the notion that life is only joyful and beautiful moment after moment, with each new high being the foreshadowing to a new goal shattered, the best friends possible, and a life of endless ease and no frustration. For some of us, we may see such posts and in response cultivate what we Buddhists call sympathetic joy—a type of joy one experiences when witnessing the joy of others. But often when we see someone performing success theater, it leads to feelings of jealousy and insufficiency.

When we post, it might be worth thinking about whether we are sharing only the good while ignoring the bad. Someone who shares a picture of herself and her husband with the caption "No bad days" or "Always easy and in love" is clearly not being truthful. Even for the best-paired couples, there are bad days. On those days, love, while it might be on the emotional landscape, is obscured to some extent by a number of much more difficult emotions. Perhaps a more honest caption would be "Despite our hardships and getting on each other's nerves, our love continues to deepen." I have a theory: if people posted honestly about their lives, they would not only gain the vaunted high number of "likes" but contribute to further connection, even offline.

The final aspect of The Vaca Sutta I'd like to tease out is the idea of posting at the right time. If we are overwhelmed and looking to experience the support of other people, we may quickly learn that social media is not the best way to gain intimate connection. In fact, posting "Worst day ever. Can't believe it!" may yield little to no response, only making us feel even more isolated and anxious. The "right time" for social media may be when we are wanting to share news with a large audience but are not particularly attached to the idea that we will have meaningful contact with them.

Which brings me to the notion that social media is not a replacement for human connection. The current head of the Kagyu lineage of Tibetan Buddhism, His Holiness the Karmapa, once said, "When you are hurt, sometimes you just want someone to hug you. A flat screen cannot hold your hand and share your pain."[15] I am writing this book in 2020, which undoubtedly will be known as the year the coronavirus pandemic shifted our global landscape. Like millions worldwide, I am working from home and my connection with friends and family is limited to Zoom calls and weekly poker games played via Google Meetup and an app. While I cherish my community dearly, these interactions do not make up for how, for months, I haven't been able to hug a loved one who is struggling. Similarly, no matter how many comments you get on something you post online, it will never be the same as someone looking you in the eyes and telling you "You're loved."

Social media has the ability to connect us with many people, so we do have a responsibility to post things that are true, kind, beneficial, offered with good intention, and shared at the right time. But if we can't keep track of these foundational teachings of the Buddha or if we are looking to connect more deeply with others, we may have to close the laptop and seek out a friend who can hold space for us and give us support as we navigate our stressful situations. As the Karmapa went on to say, "The internet places our relationships in the cloud, but we need to live our relationships here on the ground."[16] The more grounded we are—with our breath and in our bodies—the more we are able to navigate the arrows that come our way and not add stress and anxiety on top, thus leaving the second arrow behind.

CHAPTER 7

The Art of Letting Go

I suggest you follow this advice coming from the Tibetan Buddhist tradition: 'short periods, many times.'

—Dza Kilung Rinpoche, *The Relaxed Mind*[17]

Some not-so-helpful things you may already be doing about your anxiety:

» Beating yourself up for feeling it.
» Struggling against it.
» Drinking yourself numb.
» Hoping it magically goes away.
» Answering as many emails as possible, in the off chance you will receive less tomorrow.

What you can do about anxiety:

» Meditate.
» Get more sleep than you think you need.

» Eat good and nutritious food.
» Drink lots of water (You know what? Go get a glass right now. I'll wait.)
» Notice the stories you tell yourself all the time. Let. That. Shit. Go.

My honest hope is you are a few hours, days, or weeks into reading this book and have been experimenting with shamatha meditation. This is, by far, the most effective way I have found to train the mind to notice the stories it tells itself and to let them go. Yet I am not naive; you may not have sat yet. If you have, awesome! If not, perhaps today is the day?

Here are three other effective practices to help you notice your anxiety-producing storyline and relax back into the present moment.

The Hiccup Meditation

I call this practice "the hiccup meditation" because it's a slight interruption from whatever is happening to you. This technique is not going to unearth the root causes of your anxiety and transform them, but it will help you drop the storyline currently plaguing you and it will help you come back into the present moment with a bit of a "fresh start" mentality.

Ready?

Take three deep breaths in through the nose then exhale out through the mouth.

That's it.

Simple, right? I have found when I get heavily triggered, this short gap of taking these three breaths is enough for me to focus without distraction on something other than the story I'm telling myself.

Years ago, when I was moving in with my then-girlfriend (now wife), I had to go to my old apartment in Brooklyn with a U-Haul, single-handedly pack everything up, get rid of a bunch of furniture (yes, she has better taste than me), clean the place, and drive back to Queens. Yet, I had only allowed myself a few hours to do so before an important, last-minute business meeting!

Not surprisingly, I was running late by the time I climbed into the driver's seat. I took off in the truck, already noticing how my body was wracked with tension as I navigated the narrow Brooklyn streets in my oversized vehicle, only to pull onto the bridge—and immediately hit bumper-to-bumper traffic. Twenty minutes later, I wasn't much farther from where I was before and my years of meditation training began to seem like a far-off dream. Anxiety had taken over. The storylines of "I'm going to be late," "These people will never want to work with me once they realize how unprofessional I am," and "You always do this! You always over-schedule yourself" were on repeat until I had wrapped myself up in a pretty damn tight cocoon.

Then I remembered to practice. I tried to do shamatha but couldn't focus for a long period of time given the start-and-stop traffic. So, I took those three deep breaths: in through the nose, out through the mouth. Repeat. One last time.

After I had taken this momentary pause, I noticed my shoulders had returned to their normal resting posture. My stomach unknotted. I could tune back into the reality of my situation and let go of the obsessive stories that had gotten a hold of my mind. I could simply relax into the present for a moment and figure out how to act more skillfully. And guess what? The people I was supposed to meet? They ended up rescheduling on me ten minutes later! Like so many of these situations, when stress begins to run our life, the thing I was worried about wasn't even based in reality.

The Thought Party

Sometimes, people start to believe they can't meditate because they have too many thoughts. When I hear them say such a thing, I like to introduce the thought party.

I first experienced the thought party when I was in college. I was hosting a visiting Buddhist teacher I had invited to campus for a full meditation weekend. He sat down with the fledgling meditation group I had started (a room full of stressed-out over-achievers) and frowned. I admired this teacher a great deal and began to worry: Were we not up to snuff? Could he tell just how inexperienced we were? Perhaps. This teacher took one look at us and said, "Instead of starting with shamatha, let's do an experiment."

He then guided us to not resist our thoughts or struggle against them. Instead, he instructed, "Let them flow." We sat there for thirty seconds or so before he said, "More." Another minute passed. "More." Finally, we were invited to think all of the thoughts—whatever thoughts we could muster, we were told to get them going at once.

In the same vein, I invite you to try this experiment right now: Think all of your thoughts. Get them all out there.

You may initially have something to think about—your kids, your romantic relationship, that TV show you are binge-watching— but at a certain point, the tank hits empty and you're out of fuel. No thoughts. Just for an instant, you might recognize there is nothing left to think about. What relief! What relaxation! And then your mind might come up with something new.

Similar to the hiccup meditation, this technique is not going to help you change your relationship with anxiety for the long-term, but it is a good thing to try and do on occasion to remind yourself of some good news: you can indeed rest your mind, if even for an instant.

Mindfulness of Emotions

Thus far, I've emphasized practices and philosophy to help you relate to stress and suffering. But if you picked up this book, it's likely you are grappling with some pretty strong emotions caused by the very real suspicion that something is terribly wrong—either with you, your relationships, or our world right now and you want help navigating that terrain.

Sometimes, when we are confronted by strong emotions, we tend to:

» Run away from them and distract ourselves.
» Tamp them down and ignore them.
» Act out on them, in the hope doing so will get rid of them.

Let's say you're like every other human out there and at times feel lonely. Instead of attempting to investigate loneliness, your go-to mechanism is to decide it's too uncomfortable to examine, so you run away from it. Instead of letting the emotion reveal itself, you quickly go on Tinder or another dating app, scroll through Facebook or Instagram, begin online shopping, or binge-watch something on Hulu—some way (any way!) to distract yourself from the feeling itself. Yet, if you've ever done this, you know that after the next Tinder match, the half hour on social media, the shoes get bought, or the season ends, the emotion will still be there waiting to express itself.

Another way you may habitually relate to emotions is by tamping them down and hoping they will simply go away. Because you don't want to feel what you feel, you try to numb out. Maybe you pour yourself a drink or smoke something. Maybe you just keep repeating, "Not going to look at you, strong emotion." Yet, when you do this, it's a bit like the training sequence in the movie *Rocky*. I may be dating myself here, but in preparation for his big match, there's a classic eighties montage of Rocky running up and down flights of steps, jumping rope, and exercising in myriad of other ways to ultimately get bigger and better for the final match. Similarly, when you ignore your emotional state, it goes through its own *Rocky* montage because it comes back bigger and stronger than ever and eventually knocks you to your knees.

A third way you may habitually distance yourself from your emotions is to become overreactive. Sometimes, you might find yourself so uncomfortable with feeling a certain way that instead of keeping the emotion inside, you choose to act out on it in the hopes that doing so makes it somehow disappear. For example, you and your spouse got into an argument in the morning before you left for work. Physically, you're in a meeting, but mentally, you're still arguing with your partner.

The emotion has its hooks in you—you're barely present to what's going on. Yet, you know the person leading the meeting is taking up a lot of time, so even though you're angry at your spouse and not at that person, you end up snapping at them in front of everyone, asking them to wrap it up because you have other matters needing your attention. The room goes silent. Clearly, this was not a skillful way for you to relate to your emotion. Now, in addition to your anger, you might experience some shame and embarrassment and have to deal with the ramifications of acting out in such a silly way.

We need to learn a better way to relate to our emotions. On the topic of anger, the Zen master Thich Nhat Hanh once offered the perfect example: Imagine someone whose house is on fire. Instead of attempting to first put out the flames, they go running after the person who set the fire to tell them off. He wrote, "If we can take care of our own anger instead of focusing on the other person, we will get immediate relief."[18] Which brings us to the middle way between running away, tamping down, or unskillfully acting out on our emotions: feeling what we feel—without judgment.

By learning how to be with our feelings without judgment, we are applying mindfulness to our emotional state, similar to how we bring mindfulness to our breathing during shamatha practice.

Often when we experience strong emotions like fear, anxiety, and anger, the main thing we want is for them to go away. It's like you're being followed by an annoying toddler who keeps asking you, "Why?"

"Why do you think you can relax? There's a report due tomorrow."

"Why do you think you will ever meet someone? Every other relationship has ended."

"Why do you think it's okay to be worried about your finances? There are thousands of homeless refugees at your border who have nothing."

Yet, we keep trying to pick up the pace in the hopes of escaping the toddler.

In one of his earliest teachings, the Satipatthana Sutta, the Buddha taught about becoming mindful of the feeling tone underlying our emotional states. My suggestion, based on what the Buddha taught, is to turn around and look directly at the toddler. Hear what the toddler is saying. See if there is any truth to it. Simply hang out in a nonjudgmental way with the toddler for a moment and, like an actual young child, the toddler will likely calm down.

Joseph Goldstein (cofounder of the Buddhist organization the Insight Meditation Society), once gave a talk where he encouraged students to note when emotions come up and simply say to themselves, "It's okay to feel this."[19] I found this simple phrase so revolutionary. It's not "It's time for you to go away, emotions" or "I need to fix or change you, emotions." Instead, "It's okay to feel this."

When we are overwhelmed by life or the state of the world, it doesn't mean we're wrong. It's okay to feel that way. In these practices, we are discovering we don't need to beat ourselves up for having emotions. They are natural to the human state. When we are attracted to someone, we feel giddy and excited. When we fear something, we feel claustrophobic and nervous. These are okay things to feel. The trick is to allow ourselves the time and space to be with the emotion, without giving in to the desire to move away from or attempt to solve it. The following practice is based on Joseph Goldstein's advice and can also be found at lodrorinzler.com/anxiety:

» Set a timer for five or ten minutes. Take your meditation posture.

» Start off with mindfulness of the breath; tune into the body breathing, relaxing with its natural cycle. When various thoughts arise, gently acknowledge them and return to the physical sensation of the in-breath and the out-breath.

» At some point, a strong emotion may arise. This is natural.

In normal shamatha practice you would acknowledge it and return to the breath. Here, we give it space to express itself a bit.

» Allow yourself the space to feel what you feel. Mentally say to yourself, "It's okay to feel this." Notice any resistance to being with the emotion. See if you can stay with the emotion itself. When stories about the emotion arise—ways to fix the situation or what you might say to someone to defend the emotion—gently acknowledge them and let them go, returning your mindfulness of the emotion itself.

» Here, we are not trying to get rid of the feeling. We are looking directly at it. We are seeing it for what it is—a thought with a lot of energy behind it. Staying firmly grounded in your body and relying on the stabilizing influence of the breath, simply hold your seat and be with the emotion as it is.

» If the emotion changes or fades away, as it often will when we look at it, return to the breath. After the timer goes off, take three deep breaths—in through the nose and out through the mouth, just to calm the nervous system a bit. Reenter your day.

The more we look directly at our stress and anxiety, the quicker we see our way through it. In the next chapter, we learn a four-step meditation practice that allows us to recognize what we are feeling and allows some space for strong emotions to exist, so that we become inquisitive about them and ultimately move through them in a healthy way.

CHAPTER 8

A Practice for Working with Strong Emotions

From moment to moment, we can choose how we relate to our emotions. This power of choice gives us freedom, and it would be crazy not to take advantage of it.

—Pema Chödrön[20]

When it comes to working with anxiety, we need as many tools on our proverbial tool belt as possible. Building off the mindfulness of emotions practice, I will introduce you to the practice of RAIN. RAIN is a technique that was developed by Buddhist teacher Michele McDonald which I have found to be instrumental in tackling strong forms of emotions that have come up for me over the years. While different words are sometimes applied to the acronym, commonly RAIN stands for Recognize, Accept, Investigate, and Non-Identification. Let's do it together.*

---

* You can find a recording of this meditation at lodrorinzler.com/anxiety.

Begin by sitting in shamatha. Now bring your attention to a strong emotion, something already present or bubbling right beneath the surface.

Recognize it: you can place a name on the emotion if you would like such as "frustration," "sadness," "joy," or "excitement." If you sense a momentary reprieve from strong emotions, you can even ask yourself, "How am I feeling right now?" and notice what comes up. Here, we are not judging these emotions as good or bad. We are simply recognizing the emotional landscape that is present today. After a few minutes of familiarizing yourself with these emotions . . .

Accept them: simply allow yourself space to feel what you feel. Tendencies to distract yourself, tamp the emotions down, or act out on them may arise. Here, however, we are being rigorously noncorrective. Hold your seat and give yourself some room for the emotions to exist without having to do anything about them. This is not a deeply intellectual attitude; it's more an intuitive awareness, trusting yourself to the extent you can be with your emotions. There may even be a moment where notice you are waking up to who you are and are no longer trying to escape from yourself, so more relaxation may arise.

Investigate: sometimes considered "Interest," the "I" in RAIN invites us to take an interest in and get curious about our emotional state. There are numerous ways to do this, but one simple method is to ask yourself, "What is this emotion trying to show me" or "Is there some valid communication arising out of this emotion?" The tricky aspect here is that you may be tempted to engage your thinking mind and problem-solve around scenarios spinning out of this emotion. Stay curious about the emotion itself, not the stories spiraling out of it.

I was born and raised in a Tibetan Buddhist household. This tradition emphasizes looking at our emotions through an analytical lens, examining the very nature of the feeling itself. For example, you can ask yourself questions like:

Where did this emotion come from?
Where was it born?
Does it have a color? A shape? A size? A texture? A temperature?
Where does it go when I am not actively experiencing it?
Will this emotion always be here?

Sometimes, through investigating the very nature of the emotion, you may realize it is not as solid and permanent as it might appear. It is, in fact, a thought with a lot of energy behind it (like all thoughts) will arise and dissolve when given the time to do so.

Non-Identification: having acknowledged the emotion, given it space to breathe and express itself, and then having investigated it, you can gently thank it for what it taught you and you no longer identify with it. In this step, you are recognizing that you are not your emotion, which admittedly is more an attitude than an action.

If your name is Kate, for example, you are not going to now be called Angry Kate. The anger is a part of you, but you have proven that you can remain rooted long enough to encompass it without being overwhelmed by it. You don't need to become too attached to or identified with any given emotion. These emotional states are ephemeral and will change and fade over time. Like the sound of an ambulance going by, the emotion may be upsetting but won't always be a part of your present experience. One way to transition is to connect to your sense perceptions, expanding your awareness to include your environment. Alternatively, you can take three deep breaths, in through the nose and out through the mouth, transitioning you out of your practice.

Some Buddhist teachers emphasize a different word for the "N," namely "Nurture." Having spent this much time looking directly at your emotions, you might continue to feel tender or a bit sad. You could close your practice by offering yourself loving-kindness, as explained later on in this book. Alternatively, as you get up from your meditation, you can take some time to do something nourishing for yourself. It might be enjoying a warm cup of tea, calling an old friend, or having a milkshake (I like milkshakes). After this practice, whatever small gesture you consider within the realm of self-care is a good thing to do as you emerge from this hard work.

Strong emotions, including stress and anxiety, may continue to arise in your post-meditation experience. But, we have some more tools to add to the tool belt to help acknowledge the stories around those emotions and return to the present moment.

CHAPTER 9

Noting and Dismissing Storylines

One rule I have made for myself is to never say that I have anxiety. I always say that I move through anxiety . . . You are more than whatever it is you are going through.

—Cleo Wade, Where to Begin [21]

One form of meditation you may enjoy is contemplation practice. It often begins with a few minutes of shamatha to allow us to settle the mind a bit. Once we are more relaxed into the present moment, we can reflect on a question or a phrase and see what arises from our gut, intuition, or wisdom mind (however you want to refer to the little voice inside of you is fine). I want to offer three questions that can put you in touch with that more intuitive, less intellectual voice on-the-spot and help shift you away from your current anxiety. These are not formal contemplation techniques, but ways to enter into a contemplative mindset.

Is This Helpful?

One way anxiety traps us is by playing the same one to three stories on a loop. There is a great chapter in ABC News correspondent Dan Harris' book *10% Happier*. He shares his experience of being on a long meditation retreat and how, on the final day, the lead teacher encouraged the participants to remain as present as possible for the remainder of their time in retreat. Dan raised his hand and asked the question, "How can you advise us not to worry about the things we have to do when we reenter the world? If I miss my plane, that's a genuine problem." He had lots of thoughts floating around about booking a car to pick him up, packing his things, and making other arrangements. "Fair enough," the teacher replied, "but when you find yourself running through your trip to the airport for the seventeenth time, perhaps ask yourself the following question: 'Is this useful?'"

I have found "Is this useful?" as well as my personal variation "Is this helpful?" to have a profound effect on my life. For example, I could be in the shower washing my hair but, in my head, I'm locked in a back-and-forth argument with someone who (to state the obvious) isn't even present! Worse still, this isn't the first time I've played out the conversation with this person but the twenty-fifth. In that moment, it's a good opportunity to simply ask myself, "Is this helpful?" The answer that has always come back, not surprisingly, is "No." It's not helpful to prepare for a conversation I likely will never have with someone who I rarely talk to, right? Once we acknowledge that a given story we're telling ourselves isn't useful or helping us in any way, it's a lot easier to let it go.

What Can I Enjoy Right Now?

When we are able to get out of our head and relax into the present moment, we may glimpse a simple form of contentment. When you're doing the shamatha practice (Do you like how I'm now assuming you're doing it, instead of me asking you if you are?) and you are able to rest with the breath for even a few cycles of in and out, you might discover that you feel okay. In this moment of simply resting with the breath, before the next stressful thoughts arise, you might even feel more than okay—you feel good about the experience. You're present to the world around you and it's just dandy. This is what I mean when I use the word "contentment."

When we meditate regularly, we have the chance to take very ordinary things, such as drinking a glass of water, and make them extraordinary—the extra part is we are infusing the basic experience with our presence. We are there for the taste of the water and are present to how cool and refreshing it can be. Somehow, this thing that we do each day now is somewhat magical. The more you meditate regularly, the more you may be able to apply this question when you get a bit lost in anxiety: "What can I enjoy right now?"

Imagine sitting in the waiting room at a hospital. Important test results are coming your way. Even if you haven't been to the doctor in years, this image might trigger some tension in the body. But what if, in such a moment, you were able to ask yourself, "What can I enjoy right now?"

This question brings us into the present moment long enough to acknowledge our surroundings. Perhaps you see two children playing amicably across the room and it warms your heart. Maybe a song you haven't heard in years is playing through the sound system and it brings up some sweet nostalgia. Perhaps you realize you are able to move your body, or see, or hear, and it is sort of miraculous. You can enjoy any of those things if you gently invite yourself into this very moment.

What Am I Grateful for Today?

I'm a big fan of gratitude practices. In fact, every morning before I reach for my phone or swing my feet off the bed, I reflect on the question "What am I grateful for today?" My wife might still be in bed beside me, and my heart swells with gratitude for her. A cat might be climbing on me already and my menagerie of pets floats through my mind, appreciating their kindness and the simple fact that they are healthy. I look up at the ceiling and appreciate the roof over my head and the relative quiet of my apartment. I remember I'm not wearing my glasses and experience gratitude for still having my eyesight. These are pretty basic things and this whole process may only last for a minute or two but it radically transforms how I enter my day.

You could do a similar reflection when you wake up if you would like. I don't recommend trying to list a certain number of things or to make sure you force yourself to experience gratitude for things you think you "should" feel grateful for. Just allow some space around the question and see what arises within you. You are not analyzing your situation—this is a practice about listening to the inner voice that pipes up when it is given some time to be heard.

As you go about your day, this question is a helpful one to reflect upon. Perhaps you are in a meeting that seems like it will never end. In that moment, asking "What am I grateful for?" might shift you from a place of frustration to one of openness. You might look across the table and see a work colleague and experience some tenderness, recalling how they have kindly shown up for you in the past. You might glimpse someone who is going through the loss of a loved one and feel grateful that your mother is still alive. There are any number of things we can develop appreciation for, if we can return to the present moment.

With each of these questions, we have a choice: we can either stew in our anxiety or we can attempt to note when we're lost in a story, cut through it, and come into what is happening here and now. Within every moment, there is plenty for us to enjoy and appreciate. These phrases help us get there.

CHAPTER 10

The Power of Simplicity

Living simply makes loving simple. The choice to live simply necessarily enhances our capacity to love.

—bell hooks, *All About Love*

We live in a society where we are constantly instructed to want and do "more." If you have a good relationship, you ought to get married. Married? How about children? Children? You should buy a house with a yard for them! We could apply this craving for more to the technology, clothes, or the cars we buy, the jobs we pursue, and so on. At some point though, we may discern it's a good idea to simplify our lives, which starts with simplifying our minds and daily activities.

As we continue to deepen our meditation practice and apply on-the-spot techniques to relate to our anxiety, we may find that such a discernment naturally arises. Perhaps you are meditating on the breath and a thought comes up: "I really ought to call my mother."

"Thinking," you say to yourself, before returning to the breath. Your mind retorts, "You haven't called her all week."

"Thinking." A few breaths enter and then leave your body.

"You're a pretty horrible kid, you know that? Most people call their moms much more than you do."

"Thinking."

The bad news is that your mind wanders off repeatedly and you keep returning to the breath, until your mind wanders in a different direction. The good news is that after the hundredth time you have acknowledged such a thought, you will likely arise from the meditation seat pretty confident that calling your mom is a worthwhile endeavor. This is an example of discernment in action: you have gotten to see your mind in its entirety and you are learning what aspects of your life you want to cultivate and which ones you want to cut out. We can then apply those lessons to the rest of our life.

One lesson that came from my practice sparked a major shift in my life. Having lived in New York City for over a decade, I had done the thing, so to speak. I had started a successful business, been featured repeatedly in the *New York Times* for my work, married the woman of my dreams, had lots of friends and fun, social things to attend, and yet at times, I found myself a walking ball of stress. Please remember: I was a full-time meditation teacher throughout this time. I sat in meditation every day and frequently attended retreats to deepen my practice and study. I was walking the proverbial walk when it came to my meditation practice but would still get incredibly triggered by stressful situations. That's when I realized I needed to apply some discernment when it came to my environment.

As I meditated, I often noticed the sounds of our aging neighbors arguing through the thin walls. After years of this distraction (alongside the sound of construction ringing in my ears and ambulance sirens blaring as they went by, and more), I began to admit that my mind might feel less agitated if I did not live in as stressful an environment. My wife and I had recently stayed in Upstate New York in a small guesthouse on my mother's property for a few weeks. I reflected on that time and how much I enjoyed the simplicity of it. We began to discuss the idea of living a simpler life. The more I began to listen to my heart and body, the more I realized just how burned-out I was living in New York City. The constant noise, smells, and pace—while once invigorating—were now wearing me down. I needed a change.

Six months later, I made a slew of sacrifices but was living in Upstate New York. My wife could still go into the city to teach meditation and I brought most of my work online. As I write this, I'm sitting in a cozy, quiet room in Hudson, New York with the pleasant sounds of a train whistling in the background and a snoozing puppy at my feet. Having discerned New York City was now too much for my system, as painful as it was to leave, I did so and continue to feel one thousand times more at ease than ever before in my life.

I share this story not to inspire anyone to leave New York City (I maintain it's the best and most sophisticated city in the world) but to share how we may at times need to cut things out that are no longer great for us. We may need to sacrifice some of the things we are told we ought to pursue (such as chasing fame and fortune) for things that feel personally meaningful for us (such as space and self-care). For most people, the discernment coming out of meditation may not guide you to uproot your living situation but might tell you to move away from certain habits or behaviors. You may realize that:

» You spend too much time staring at the news.
» There are some people in your life who are not very good to you.
» You need boundaries between your work and home life.
» You buy more clothes than you could possibly wear.
» You feel drained after spending all day looking at screens.

When we take the time to quiet the mind, there are a thousand things we can learn about simplicity and how we may want to change our life.

While I'm not a fan of how the wellness industry sometimes conducts itself, I do appreciate the need for self-care. Self-care means different things to different people. For me, it means eating nutritious foods, prioritizing enough hours of sleep, exercising, and yes, you guessed it, meditating. These seem like no-brainers, right? Yet, let me ask you: when was the last time you did all four in one day?

We might sleep in and feel good about the lack of bags under our eyes only to realize we no longer have time to go to the gym. Or we work out and are feeling great but binge on junk food because, well, we burned those calories already, didn't we? I'm damn confident that if you did all four of these things in one day— eat well, sleep well, meditate, and exercise—you would experience more clarity and energy that would help you address the stressful situations in your life.

By offering those four activities, there's an implicit nudge toward looking at your life and seeing what might need to be eliminated in order to simplify and have time and space to care for yourself. Baked into this notion of self-care is knowing your own triggers (clearly, some of mine are arguing neighbors and sirens) and establishing boundaries around them to the best of your ability.

Sometimes, meditation students come to me because they are bombarded by the nonstop news cycle. When I hear this complaint, I am reminded of something the author bell hooks once wrote: "Were we, collectively, to demand that our mass media portray images that reflect love's reality, it would happen. This change would radically alter our culture."[22] Instead, mass media is stuck on portraying images of violence, which feeds into our subconscious and dominates our minds. I get how it can be hard to avoid if you work somewhere which has the television on 24/7 but for most of us, this is a matter of needing to set clear boundaries around what we do with our time.

If you're the sort of person who has CNN text them alerts about breaking tragedies, flips the television on the moment you get home to hear the news in the background, or takes every bathroom break at work to check Twitter, I have to break it to you: you're causing yourself more anxiety than needed. Thich Nhat Hanh put it best when he pointed out, "Any time we have leisure, we want to invite something else to enter us, opening ourselves to the television and telling the television to come and colonize us."[23] He's right: we're asking for stressful situations to take over our body and mind! In order to care for ourselves better, we may need to practice simplicity by cutting out such toxic influences.

I am by no means saying that anyone should ignore the news of the day; it's important to stay informed by a wide variety of sources in order to enrich our understanding of the world we live in. Yet at times, the nonstop news cycle can indeed colonize our brain and it may no longer be helpful to be exposed to a parade of constant suffering. Along those lines, one trick I learned a while back is to turn off notifications on my phone. I've gone so far in this direction, I don't even get a buzz when someone texts me. You have to call in order to bring me out of what I want to be focusing on and into distraction and, potentially, stress. The end result is I tend to my phone when I want to, as opposed to constantly being served triggers on a platter.

If you suspect your usage of your phone, television, or Internet scrolling is causing you more angst than is useful, it's time to establish some boundaries. There are a gazillion apps and websites built to help monitor your phone and Internet usage and shut down certain apps or block certain sites after a preset amount of time. You too can turn off a slew of notifications if they no longer serve you. You can stop following social media accounts that trigger anxiety in you and focus your attention on those that breed positivity and support. If you're obsessive like me, you could even schedule the times you respond to email in order to not constantly be looking at your phone for every incoming "Maybe this will freak me out" message. You can move your television remote somewhere out of the way, thus cutting through the habitual impulse to simply turn the television on because it's there.

Take a moment to consider how much time you actually want to spend exposing yourself to the news and other triggers. Really truly—take two minutes right now to discern what that amount of time would be. Once you determine this figure, commit to it as your media diet. Like a food diet, you will need to apply some discipline and limit yourself to just what you say you want to do. You can track it on an old-school notebook if you'd like. You can enjoy the time thoroughly and educate yourself about the issues of the day. Yet, when that time has elapsed, you need to apply the discipline to stop. You'll be happy you did.

Meditation is a helpful tool to physiologically rewire the brain. Yet, if you get up off your meditation seat and are surrounded by stressful triggers, it will be hard to maintain any semblance of mindfulness. If you look at how best to simplify those post-meditation hours, cutting out some of the harmful tendencies you may take for granted, you'll be surprised by how much more mental space you have for the positive things you can do.

In this section, we have reviewed our relationship with stress and anxiety and have developed a hefty tool belt full of practices that can be employed to relate to these strong emotions. To work with the mind, we can do my favorite practice—shamatha—to slice through the cocoon of the stories that keep us closed off from the world around us. We can relate more fully to our emotions through practices like RAIN, learning that it's okay for us to feel what we feel, right now in the moment. In our post-meditation experience, we can consider the traps that prevent us from connecting to the present whether that is social media inciting comparing mind or the identity markers we cling to that separate us from other people, and simplify, letting the toxic parts of our lives go.

The more present we are in the body, on or off the meditation seat, the more we begin to connect to the world around us. As bell hooks pointed out at the top of this chapter, the more simply we live, the more capacity we have to love. In the next section, we begin to explore what it means to engage our interpersonal relationships and society overall from a loving and open heart. If the bad news is that there is no magic button we can push to eliminate stressful situations, the good news is that stress is not our natural state. We're actually, in fact, basically good.

PART TWO

The Good News: You Can Relax

CHAPTER 11

Discovering Our Basic Goodness

Suffering is not enough.

—Thich Nhat Hanh, *Being Peace*

I've focused on the bad news: anxiety exists (sorry). It shows up as this veil that separates us from the world around us and sometimes it feels like that veil is impossible to lift. The other day, I got an email from a meditation student of mine who went to the doctor after facing some pretty horrible circumstances. The diagnosis in the half-hour consult? "You will be anxious for the rest of your life." No wonder she wrote to me, terrified. Telling someone that they will always be anxious is only going to make them more anxious.

While anxiety may be a part of the fabric of your life at this time, you can mitigate your relationship to it through meditation and lessening the stressful triggers in your day-to-day existence. Maybe you read the simplicity chapter, quit your job and relationships, grabbed a remarkably large supply of canned food, and have already hightailed it to a cave in the woods. If you haven't though, you will probably need to contemplate how you will navigate your existent stressors. To be frank, if you are reading this in a cave, I'm guessing you will find there are new stressors, like the temperature fluctuation or the fear of bears visiting you in your sleep. No matter where you are, stressful triggers will arise, whether you're meditating or not.

The good news, of course, is that meditation can help us acknowledge our anxious thoughts, see them as the ephemeral gnats that they are, and let them go.

Now here's the best news: you are not an inherently anxious person. You can, in fact, relax. The careless words from the doctor notwithstanding, no one is in for a lifetime of constant anxiety. Yes, I realize you may have come to wear the identity of an anxious person—you have not known much else for a very long time—but this identity marker is actually just the top layer of who you truly are. You are, instead, inherently good.

When we meditate, we don't just get familiar with our neuroses, be they jealousy, fear, or even shame; we also discover our innate wisdom. In Tibetan Buddhism, we call this basic goodness. It's the sanity right there beneath the surface, our own vulnerable and tender core of humanity waiting to emerge so we can benefit ourselves and others. Everyone possesses basic goodness and the more we relax into the present moment, the more we are able to discover it for ourselves.

This is probably the most important term in the book so let me break it down. *Basic* is not like "basic bitch," implying uncouth. It means goodness is inherent and fundamental to all of us. We don't need to go out and get this goodness; it's basic to who we are in this moment. *Goodness* is not related to some Star Wars-esque battle between good and evil. There are no "basically bad" people for us to fight against. "Goodness" implies a sense of wholeness. We are primordially and completely okay—there is nothing wrong with us or in need of fixing.

If you just breathed a sigh of relief, you're not alone; the notion of basic goodness is powerful and countercultural. We are taught from a young age that there is something wrong with us, that we need to do more, be more, and accomplish more—it's exhausting. When we buy into the mentality of always needing "more," we can never relax into the moment and appreciate who we are. We're instead looking ahead to who we could be.

This often means we're eyeing the next step in life: the next rung on the ladder to climb for our education, which could hopefully lead to a good job, which could lead to a good financial situation, which could lead to a good home, which could create space for a good family, and so on. We are constantly presented with more things we ought to do in the search of goodness instead of looking for it within.

So, to beat the dead horse, the best news I can offer is pretty damn great: we can realize that we are inherently good, whole, and complete as we are. We don't need a lot of external factors to make us whole—we can experience that wholeness right here and now.

Please don't take my word for it though. If you want to rage against me and say "People are shit, myself included," be my guest. Yet at some point, while you were meditating, I'm assuming you were able to relax with the breath for just a few moments and in that slight gap you realized, "Huh. I'm okay right now." This moment—where we notice that underneath the maelstrom of intrusive thoughts, we are basically good—is one of the most powerful moments in meditation. The Tibetan Buddhist teacher Chögyam Trungpa Rinpoche once said, "We experience glimpses of goodness all the time, but we often fail to acknowledge them. When we see a bright color, we are witnessing our own inherent goodness. When we hear a beautiful sound, we are hearing our own basic goodness. When we step out of the shower, we feel fresh and clean, and when we walk out of a stuffy room, we appreciate the sudden whiff of fresh air. These events may take a fraction of a second, but they are real experiences of goodness."[24]

Catching a glimpse of basic goodness is where the beautiful part of meditation begins. Having meditated for thirty-plus years now, here's the entirety of the path as I understand it, given my limited capabilities:

1. Discover your basic goodness.
2. Develop confidence in your basic goodness.
3. Continuously see the world through the lens of your basic goodness.

That's it. If you have even had the tiniest moment in meditation where you relaxed into your natural state and felt a glimpse of goodness, please check item number one off your list. However, the majority of the time spent on the spiritual path is learning to trust that experience, to learn to accept who we are, moment by moment. The more we do this work, the more we are able to connect to others and the world around us from a place of basic goodness as opposed to one of stress and anxiety.

It is not just you and me who are basically good—it's everyone. Every single person possesses basic goodness, which means that the person who cut you off in traffic is basically good. Your ex is basically good. Your difficult boss is basically good. And yet, these people sort of act like jerks at times. Oddly enough, both can be true!

If you are exploring this notion of basic goodness (or better yet, have experienced it to some degree), then you know there are times when you are in touch with your inherent goodness and wisdom and other times, not so much. You would love to constantly manifest basic goodness, but lo and behold, the telemarketer who called you as you were running out the door just pissed you off and you snapped at them. This is an example of you, basic goodness and all, still sometimes acting from a confused state, one where you are more in touch with your neurosis than your wakefulness.

I bring this up not to shame you but to point out how you and I can possess basic goodness *and* still sometimes act from a place of confusion. Good lord, I know I have. Knowing how I can at times be unskillful allows me to give other people more of a break when they do the same.

Let's pretend you're stuck in traffic during your morning commute. Your gaze falls on a frustrated gentleman in the next car over who is muttering to himself and slamming his fists on the steering wheel. Instead of closing your heart off or turning the other way, what if you have a moment of recognition: "Oh, this person is late for work and angry about traffic, just like me." Or you see an overwhelmed clerk at a department store who is snapping at customers, rushing around like a chicken with its head cut off. In that moment you realize, "This person is having a rough day, just like me." The fact that these people are acting mad or sad or any number of ways does not negate their inherent goodness, right?

not worthy of love. Not good enough. Not together enough. Not capable of being loved. Everyone else? Sure. You? Not so much. I've seen it hundreds of times, each letter written in a different way and communicating the belief that the author is simply not enough. This is one manifestation of what we can call the trap of doubt.

The trap of doubt is the primary obstacle blocking us from continuously resting in our basic goodness. Maybe you're meditating and you glimpse that you are okay—just for a minute—with the breath, resting firmly in the present moment. But then a thought arises: "You jerk. You don't get to rest. You need to do more than this! You're wasting time." Or better yet: "You're a waste of time." Doubt has reared its ugly head yet again.

According to my tradition, doubt can manifest in six ways. The first will seem strikingly familiar (hello anxiety, I see you) but the other aspects of doubt arise frequently when we are cut off from our innate sense of wholeness.

1. Anxiety

Think about the refrain from Simon & Garfunkel's "The Sound of Silence" when they sing "Hello darkness, my old friend/I've come to talk with you again." When you don't get enough sleep or are experiencing a significant increase in stressful triggers, anxiety will naturally come to talk with you again, an old friend seeking some of your time.

From a Buddhist point of view, anxiety arises when you fall into the trap of doubt. You question whether, at your core, you are basically good or whole as is, and thus, buy into the notion that if you could only attain this new thing out there, you would be happy. This new thing may be a perfect partner, job, kid, home, or exercise routine. It can be anything. If we get curious about our experience, we realize we're always craving for something new, something more, which will make us whole. And when we don't attain that thing? We feel anxious and crave it more. When we do attain that thing? We get anxious and crave something new.

For example, you might be seeking a promotion at work. You freak out about it for a whole month: if you get it, you could afford to move out of the place where you have roommates, which would be lovely. If you don't get it, it probably means they don't value you at work. Now that you have established a good number of stories for yourself to obsess over, you spend all your free time being anxious about this issue.

Then you get the big news: you got it! Amazing! Congratulations! After a slight pause you think, "Oh no. How am I going to break the news to my roommates? They will be devastated!" or "Moving is so stressful—I can't believe I have to go look at places on my own!" Your mind has already found something new to be anxious about.

Alternatively, you don't get the promotion. I'm sorry. After a slight pause, you think, "Is this a dead-end job? Do I need to quit?" or "Something must be wrong with me. They'll fire me soon and I'll end up on the street!" Your mind has similarly found new things to be anxious about.

I'm here to tell you that you can look anxiety in the eyes and not run from it. You don't have to spin out those stories. You can sit with the emotion, let it move through you *sans* repetitive thinking, and return to the present moment. The ability to be with our current experience—good, bad, or ugly—and remain rooted in our basic goodness? This is what we're training for during meditation.

2. Jealousy

Your coworkers go out to lunch without you and you wonder why you were not invited. Did you do something wrong? Are you not popular? Fears about being picked last at kickball in the second-grade pop up, and lo and behold, you have let yourself go straight to the conclusion that something must fundamentally be wrong with you. Instead of freaking out in anxiety though, your self-doubt manifests here as jealousy: *"Everyone else was invited. Why not me?"*

When the world doesn't treat us in the way we expect it to, we end up disappointed and, in some cases, experience envy toward those people over there who we perceive have it much better than we do. We don't feel whole and complete in ourselves so we get jealous of the person who has more money, or is married while we're single, or has a house while we're stuck in a crummy apartment. When we begin comparing ourselves to others, it brings us no joy.

One antidote, when lost in jealousy, is to remember that everyone is suffering in some way. The person who has a lot of money may also be lonely a lot of the time. The person who is married? They may be struggling to pay their bills. The beautiful house? Falling apart inside and stressing everyone out. No one has their act completely together, so we have to remember that these people may not display their issues openly and we should have kindness toward those we are jealous of, because their issues are definitely there.

3. Forgetfulness

Sometimes, when you are so lost in the stories that you tell yourself about how you're not enough, you may then lose track of the details of your life. You spiral and it takes up so much of your mental energy that there is none left to acknowledge what is happening in the present moment.

For example, have you ever walked into a room, lost in your own head, looked up, and realized you have no clue why you even went there in the first place? Well, this is self-doubt manifesting as forgetfulness. You are so closed off from the reality of your situation and so lost in your inner monologue that you can move from room to room not even remembering what you are meant to be doing in any of them.

To counter the symptom of forgetfulness, it's a good idea to slow the f*ck down. Walk slower. Take the time to sip your beverage and taste it. Notice your surroundings. The act of physically slowing down might help bring you back into the present moment, where you can once more reconnect to your own basic goodness, pulling yourself out of the trap of doubt and the subsequent forgetfulness.

4. Arrogance

Imagine the most arrogant person you know. Instead of getting lost in the emotions around what a jerk they are, take a moment to consider this: is it possible they might be overcompensating for a lack of confidence?

When you don't feel very good about yourself, you might have a tendency to puff yourself up to make up for the big black hole of doubt you're experiencing. Instead of looking directly at your sense of doubt, you spend your mental energy telling yourself that you're right and anyone who disagrees with you is wrong, or how you are smarter or better than those people you're having an issue with. This can, frankly, be exhausting.

When you notice that you are manifesting doubt as a form of arrogance you can ask yourself a question: "Is that so?" Is it so that other people's arguments have no valid points? That you know better than everyone around you? Is this 100 percent true? Somehow, becoming gently inquisitive with our experience loosens our arrogance and makes us more open to other people's perspectives, bringing us back to a place of understanding and compassion.

5. Slander

When someone doesn't feel very good about themselves, they will try to put other people down to bring them to their level.

I don't think I have to say too much here: you either have acted or know someone who acts in this manner. People who are genuinely connected to basic goodness do not go out of their way to throw shade at other people; they try to use their speech to lift other people up.

Becoming more mindful of our speech is a surefire way to yank ourselves out of negative patterns. You can take one day, for example, and just monitor how you talk about others. Do your words generally praise and benefit others? Or do they drain the energy of yourself or others? If the latter, you can apply some discipline to bring yourself back to a place of using your speech as a tool for good.

6. No Synchronization between Mind and Body

You are running around your house, lost in your own head, and somehow this is the moment—the only moment really—when your clothes snag on the door. You rip your favorite sweater (which is irreplaceable) and now you're stressed-out about that too. Why? Well, when you get completely mired in doubt about your own worth and goodness, you may find yourself physically out of sorts.

Someone who is grounded in their own sense of being okay generally has a natural ease and energy to them. The Tibetan word would be *ziji*, which can be translated as "confidence," but a more direct version would be "radiating splendor." When you are in touch with basic goodness, you radiate a sense of warmth and grace. When you are disconnected from it, you are also disconnected from your body and end up tripping on the sidewalk, dropping water glasses, and stubbing your toe.

Thankfully, all of these symptoms of doubt can be treated. The prescription is none other than what I have talked about before: noticing the stories we tell ourselves, letting them go, and returning to the somatic experience of the present moment. When we return to our breath, the movement of the body, or when we listen to the conversation at hand, we may find a moment of relaxation. In this moment of peace, we are in touch with an experience of being whole and complete. Through meditation practice, we can train ourselves to unhinge the trap of doubt and return to freedom from anxiety, moment by moment.

CHAPTER 13

Awakening Your Open Heart

So you try to appeal to the goodness of every human being.
And you don't give up. You never give up on anyone.

—Representative John Lewis,
On Being with Krista Tippett [26]

One surefire way to let go of the anxiety-producing storylines in our head is to turn our attention to the people around us. One of my first Buddhist teachers was fond of saying, "If you want to be miserable, think only of yourself. If you want to be happy, think of others." This fundamental switch frees up our mental energy from over-focusing on problems which may have no current solution and opens us to the world around us.

There is a term in Sanskrit that communicates this human potential to connect with others: *bodhichitta*. *Bodhi* can be translated as "open" or "awake" while *chitta* refers to our heart/ mind. (There's not a lot of distinction between the heart and mind in this context.) All together, bodhichitta refers to our innate human ability to open and wake up our heart so that we may be more in touch with others.

Everyone has a soft spot within them, an openness and tenderness waiting to be revealed. Remember the time you were walking down the street and that puppy did that absolute puppy-like thing and your heart just melted? This is the soft spot I'm talking about. It's love for love's sake. It's not that you're romantically attracted to and want to date a dog, right? It's that you just experience love, as is. At this stage, having grounded ourselves in the foundational teachings of working with our own mind, we're moving to a new stage: the Mahayana path. *Maha* can be translated as "greater" and *yana* as "path" or "vehicle." In moving from the head to the heart, from anxiety to bodhichitta, we are essentially shifting the focus from just on us and our personal issues to one of greater connection to the world around us.

In any given moment, you can make a choice: you can perpetuate the anxiety-producing stories in your head or momentarily raise your gaze and connect with what else is happening right under your nose. When you take even these tiny vacations from your anxiety to check out your environment, there is often something you can connect with that is a gateway to opening the heart: a mother caring for her child, two friends reconnecting and hugging for way too long, a sobbing man and another person gently holding his hand. The good and bad of the world is waiting to wake up your heart, if you can lift your veil of anxiety for a moment.

The number one thing preventing you from remaining open-hearted may very well be your fear of being hurt. This could be a romantic thing, where you have put your heart on the table before and a partner has walked up with a comically large mallet and smashed it to pieces. At that point, you may have scooped up your innards and thought, "I'll just close myself off from this level of vulnerability—never again for me." You can wall up your heart, wrapping yourself in your cocoon, acting from a place of fear.

This closed-heartedness doesn't necessarily have to be a romantic thing. It could be a business endeavor. Years ago, I was working quite closely with someone and we had a beautiful habit of mentioning when we perceived the other person was operating from a place of fear. One of us might express concern about losing out on an opportunity and the other would gently ask, "Are we acting from a place of openness or from a place of fear?" Even posing the question would move us back to a place of bodhichitta, wanting to approach our work from a sense of vast potential to help others as opposed to approaching our work from a closed-off or fearful mind.

We may begin to notice that when we close our hearts, anxiety follows, as does the villainization of other people. When we villainize other people, shutting our hearts off to them, we are harming ourselves and the world around us. True peace, internally and for society overall, will not be achieved by shuttering our hearts to certain types of people, leading to us trying to systematically rid them from our lives. No, true peace will come from softening our hearts and including even the difficult people around us as part of our compassion practice.

A funny thing happened when I interviewed people for my last book, *Love Hurts: Buddhist Advice for the Heartbroken*. Well, a few funny things. One was that I thought everyone who came to meet with me and share their heartbreak story would want to talk about their ex but in fact, many people were experiencing heartbreak about the state of the world and considered themselves very alone in feeling that way. The other funny thing is that when those people who sat with me did talk about their ex, they would go through a transformation.

To be clear: I wasn't there to counsel anyone. My job was to simply sit and listen. I'd ask the question, "What is your experience of heartbreak?" and shut up. We had twenty minutes together and sometimes the other person would consider that first question and just spend our time answering it. They would tell me about how they loved their ex, and then the horrible things the ex had done, and what a jerk the ex was—and then something would shift.

They would soften toward this person. When they were given a lot of time and space to simply verbalize their emotions and be heard in a nonjudgmental manner, they would take someone they had once thought to be a lover and then saw as an enemy and ultimately end up feeling sorry for them. Our time together often concluded with, "They're a horrible prick and they deserve so many bad things—but I hope they ultimately find happiness."

I have found when I close my heart off to someone, it causes me only pain and anxiety right up until the same moment when I can soften to them. Meanwhile, the other person isn't perking up midday, interrupting a conversation and saying, "Sorry, I have to go feel bad about myself. Someone on the other side of the country is thinking negative thoughts about me." When I sit and stew about what a jerk someone is being, I am only creating more aggression in my own heart and mind. The more mental energy I spend in the realm of aggression, the more the outer world seems mad and scary to me.

A helpful Buddhist framework when considering the notion of bodhichitta is that of body, speech, and mind. If our heart/mind is open, our speech will naturally be compassionate and our activities and bodily deeds will follow suit. If our heart/mind is closed, we will perpetuate negative patterns in our speech and actions. In other words, when we spend a lot of mental energy lost in this dualistic notion of "me" versus "them," these thoughts turn into speech and deeds, which ultimately harm us and others.

If we look directly at our strong emotions and the tendency to disconnect from our bodhichitta, we will be well-prepared to deal with the people in our lives who are absolute assholes. (Once we start using terms like "asshole," by the way, it's an indication that we may have shut our heart off from them, instead of including them in our bodhichitta.) In her book *Braving the Wilderness*, Brené Brown points out, "People are hard to hate close-up." Often when we have gotten to the point of thinking of someone as our enemy, it's because we have not seen them in person or been subjected to their presence for a long period of time.

Try this thought exercise: bring to mind someone you think is a complete jerk or you don't think is worthy of your compassion. Now, map out their day: What do they do when they get up? Are they kind to their spouse? Do they play with their children? Do they kick their dog, or do they take good care of her? Continue to mentally follow them: Do they get frustrated in traffic? Do they tip the barista at their local coffee shop? Do they have projects fall apart at work? Keep following them until nighttime, letting them get tucked into bed. All told, this could be a five-minute exercise.

Even though you're doing this from the comfort of your own home and not literally shadowing them, you might have moments where you start to see a point of connection and your heart begins to relax and soften. You might think, "I also get angry when I am running late for work" or "They're just trying to provide for their loved ones, just like me." These glimpses of "just like me," are the moments we reconnect to bodhichitta, the vulnerable and raw, loving heart that's been waiting to be rediscovered.

A less theoretical exercise would be to actually spend a full afternoon with the person you find so difficult. You likely would see their concern for their spouse, their very human frustrations, and their suffering overall. When we see the pain that everyone— *everyone*—experiences, it becomes very hard to hate them and consider them as "other."

Othering someone is a fundamentally aggressive act. When we label someone as "other," we are saying that we are right, they are wrong, and they do not deserve to be treated as fully human. In my experience, it is so painful to be othered, to be met by someone else's closed heart, and I am guessing you have felt such pain as well. Here are three tools that will help us cut through the impulse to shut the heart down to those difficult people:

1. Mindfulness

Okay I'm beating a dead horse here. Thich Nhat Hanh is fond of talking about how we can "sponsor our anger" with mindfulness. He wrote,

> Usually when people are angry, they say and do things which cause damage to others and themselves. There are people who speak and act in ways which wound others. They believe that doing so will release the field of angry energy which is burning in their hearts. They shout and scream, beat things, and

shoot poisoned arrows of speech at others. These
methods of release are dangerous. . . . Therefore
the method of mindful observation in order to see
and to understand the roots of our anger is the
only method that has lasting effectiveness.[27]

If we are regularly practicing meditation, there is a gap that
occurs in our experience between feeling what we feel and acting
on it. This gap, when we can rest in it, is the difference between
launching those poisoned arrows of speech at others and doing the
internal work to transmute anger into sympathy. We can experience
whatever is coming up, remain present to it without judgment, and
then once we have calmed down, respond to other people in an
ultimately more compassionate manner.

The reason I mention sympathy is because we might, having
rested with our emotions, realize that the person who has made us
suffer is undoubtedly suffering as well. If it is helpful, before talking
to this person who stirs up such strong emotions in you, you could
ask yourself, "Do I think this person is in pain?" or "Do I think this
person is coming from the best version of themselves?" Doing so
might cut through the dualistic "me" versus "them" tendency and
help you see in that moment the one thing you may connect on is
that you are both suffering. When we realize I am suffering and you
are suffering, sympathy and compassion can bloom.

2. Remembering the Basic Goodness of Another

It is easy, when you write someone off in your heart, to say that
everyone has basic goodness—except for them. But hopefully at this
point you know this notion is not true. Everyone possesses the seed

for awakening in their hearts, but not everyone has been exposed to opportunities to water it. Remember to practice considering the hardships this person has faced and see if that helps soften your heart toward them.

We are not giving them a hall pass for bad behavior here, but acknowledging that underneath the thick veil of confusion, fear, and anger they may be wearing, there is someone who has the same potential for waking up to their own heart/mind that we do. One contemplation which may prove helpful is thinking about them as a small child. I don't know of any small children who have already hardened their hearts to the world or are explicitly biased against a particular color, creed, or type of human. They are innocent and open to experiencing the world as is. This same openness exists within the person we may call "enemy."

3. Seeing Good Qualities in Another

If we are very stuck, one simple act that could help get us unstuck is contemplating even one good quality in someone we perceive as having great character flaws. On the show *How I Met Your Mother*, there is a character named Artillery Arthur, a particularly brutal boss at the law firm where one of the main characters works. Not knowing how to work with his anger arising from his personal life, Artillery Arthur goes off like a canon at his subordinates. Also, Arthur really loves his dog and the moment the dog is brought up, he drops his anger and becomes almost baby-like in demeanor.

While Arthur is an extreme version of what I am talking about, the idea here is that everyone has redeemable qualities. Your enemy might be romantic with his partner, kind to his neighbors, or spend time volunteering coaching inner-city youth. In each of the three practice experiences mentioned in this chapter, I am recommending we are looking directly at this person long enough to acknowledge the totality of their humanity, so that we can wake up our own stubborn heart.

I've talked about the danger of closing our heart off and how it can lead to villainizing others, but so many of our world's problems stem from this tendency to disconnect from bodhichitta. When we harden our hearts to certain types of people, tribalism is born. My camp is the good camp, because we subscribe to these beliefs. Your camp is bad because your beliefs are different. This plays out as religious strife, political gridlock, race wars, and more. Whole groups of people become labeled as "other" and from there, all we want to do is close our hearts to anyone like them. This leads to so much pain in our society.

When I was eight years old, a family friend, Sonya, took me for a walk. She asked how school was and in response I said, "Well, the boys hate the girls and the girls hate the boys." Surely, this wasn't the case—the girls and the boys teased one another and within a year or two, those same individuals who hated each other ended up confessing crushes for one another. Yet, during the walk, this woman took me by the shoulder and turned me toward her. She looked me in the eyes and said, "Hate is a very strong word. You should never use the word hate."

From that day forward, I've made it a point to look closely at this particular word. I do not harbor hate in my heart for anyone, but I know people who do, and it is so painful for them. It's a lens through which they view the world, obscuring their joy and contentment. When emotions like fear or anger get solidified into a pattern such as hate, it empowers individuals to act in monstrous, horrible ways, sometimes leading to death.

On the flip side, I am inspired by heroes like Representative John Lewis, a civil rights activist who never let himself succumb to hate, no matter how much he was persecuted. As he fought for the rights of African-Americans, he was intimidated, attacked, and abused. He once said,

> We, from time to time, would discuss if you see someone attacking you, beating you, spitting on you, you have to think of that person—years ago, that person was an innocent child, innocent little baby. And so what happened? Something go wrong? Did the environment? Did someone teach that person to hate, to abuse others? So you try to appeal to the goodness of every human being. And you don't give up. You never give up on anyone.[28]

It would be so easy for someone who experienced so much harm to harden his heart and dismiss white people for the pain he experienced. Instead, Representative Lewis said, "No. These are people. I am a person. I can find common ground." I am moved that he went so far as to contemplate not just the actions the person was perpetuating today but also how they ended up there at all. The fact that he and others he worked with would wonder about the pain their abusers had experienced feels like such a big stretch of the heart to me, yet because he has done it, I know it is possible for us to do the same.

Following in the footsteps of great heroes, we can appeal to the innate goodness of every person out there. Every human being possesses basic goodness, not just you and me, which means even if we see certain types of people doing certain types of things we don't agree with, we can avoid the suffering of tribalism and instead soften our hearts to recognize their humanity. Just because they are different than us or acting confused does not mean we can give up on them. We never have to give up on anyone.

It is a profound experience when we realize that those who we consider evil or villains could benefit from our compassion. It transmutes the situation from "me versus you" to "We're all doing the best we can." Now that we have been working to train the mind to acknowledge and release its anxious stories, we can train the heart to include those beings who cause us anxiety. We can apply what are known as the Four Immeasurables, ways of offering love, so that our bodhichitta flows in ways we may never have thought possible.

CHAPTER 14

The Four Immeasurables

*The word 'love' is most often defined as a noun, yet all the
more astute theorists of love acknowledge that we would all
love better if we used it as a verb.*

—bell hooks, *All About Love* [29]

While I realize the Four Immeasurables may sound like a 1970s
opening act for Earth, Wind & Fire, they are in fact four ways
we can manifest love out of our open and awake heart/mind—our
bodhichitta. When it comes to anxiety, we're always looking to "do"
something about it. We want to fix it or to make a plan so it goes
away. While in the first section of the book I focused on managing
those stories in the mind, now we shift our focus to open-hearted
love as an antidote to stress and anxiety and specifically viewing
love as a verb, as something we can do.

When we turn our attention to our open and loving heart,
we experience just how vast it is. So vast, anxiety may arise and
dissolve against its backdrop without us having to do much about

it. When we are focused on love, these stressful storylines move through us, not unlike clouds moving across the blue sky. The clouds come and go, but the sky remains. The same can be said for our anxiety, which arises and dissolves over time, while our bodhichitta is always available to us, waiting to be rediscovered.

In the Buddhist tradition, this moment of waking up to love is considered quite beautiful. The Buddha himself spoke about the *brahma-viharas*. "Vihara" can be translated from Sanskrit as "abode" or sometimes it has been translated as "attitude" while "brahma" can be translated as "divine" or "sublime." Generally, the brahma-viharas are termed the "four immeasurables" or "four limitless qualities" although a more direct translation may be the "sublime attitudes." They are four ways we can unconditionally offer love to ourselves and others, especially in the midst of stressful circumstances.

When we see our world through the lens of an open heart, these four qualities naturally manifest as activities we can do. We find that we are less stuck on the anxiety of the day and more available to help the people around us. Over the next few chapters, I will explore these four qualities in depth, beginning with *maitri*, loving-kindness. *Maitri* can be translated as "friendliness" or "benevolence" but my favorite translation is "kind friendliness." In essence, we are are saying that the root of love is friendship. It is something to be done, a verb and not a noun, as bell hooks points out at the top of this chapter. We have to learn to act kindly to ourselves and others, in order to let anxiety go and let our love flow.

CHAPTER 15

Letting Love Flow

Sustaining a loving heart, even for the duration of the snap of a finger, makes one a truly spiritual being.

—Sharon Salzberg, *Loving-Kindness: The Revolutionary Art of Happiness* [30]

In a story dating back to the time of the Buddha, a group of monks sought his advice about where they should meditate. He used his wisdom powers (this is actually how people often talk about it. I'm not even kidding) and said, "You know where you ought to go? There is a place in the foothills of the Himalayas." So they set off to spend about four months during the rainy season in what appeared to be an ideal spot. It's said the land "appeared like a glittering blue quartz crystal: it was embellished with a cool, dense, green forest grove and a stretch of ground strewn with sand . . . " [31] It came complete with benefactors who would provide them food and care for them—what more could they ever want? Complete enlightenment seemed guaranteed. The monks each set up camp to practice under one of the trees.

The one thing the monks did not account for was the deities who lived in the aforementioned trees. These beings (and you can choose to believe there were beings or not, I am 0 percent offended if you don't) initially deferred to the monks who were there but when they didn't go away, they realized their homes had been invaded.

These tree deities began playing tricks on the monks, making horrible screeching noises and creating really terrible smells to the point where the monks were too frightened to meditate and left. The monks went back to the Buddha who, in his infinite wisdom, scanned the whole of India with his mind and was like, "Nope, actually that's the best place for you to deepen your practice—in the scary place." He sent them back to this land with a teaching known as the Karaniya Metta Sutta, sometimes referred to as the Discourse on Loving-kindness.

Instead of telling his monks to trounce those indigenous tree deities or to meditate elsewhere, the Buddha offered a valuable teaching: go to the place that scares you and hold your goddamn seat. If you're humble, gentle, and genuinely wish for the happiness and ease of others, then you can utilize these difficult, anxiety-producing circumstances as the quickest route to your own awakening. In particular, I want to point out this phrase from the Buddha's teaching:

Even as a mother protects with her life
Her child, her only child,
So with a boundless heart
Should one cherish all living beings . . .[32]

The Buddha did not send these monks to go play nice with these beings who were hassling them; he said they needed to cherish them in the same way a mother would protect her only child. *Wow.* Sometimes loving-kindness practice, because it's so heart-oriented is considered "hippie stuff," but when we look at the words of the Buddha, it's quite a fierce practice—it's about loving all beings with the same adamant care of a parent protecting their only kid.

What happened when the monks returned to this land with an open heart? The deities were won over by their warm feelings and actually welcomed the monks back and protected them. The two sides who perceived one another as enemies were now allies and respected each other because of the transformative practice of loving-kindness. And, as promised by the Buddha, these monks woke up their minds and hearts in supreme ways and were able to help many beings.

The moral of this story transcends whether or not you believe in tree deities. In these stories, we can think of demons and deities as actual beings or simply the challenges we have internally. We all have internal demons who might end up screeching horribly when we sit down to meditate, although the screeching might sound specifically like, "You're a loser and no one will ever love you!" or "Everyone knows about your secret shame!" The practice of loving-kindness begins with offering love to ourselves, including our internal demons, and then opens us up to offering love to others. As illustrated in the story, the root of love for self and others is friendship. You must befriend yourself before you can fully and genuinely love other people.

Okay . . . But What is Loving-Kindness/ Why Will it Help with My Anxiety?

Before we get into the practice itself, let's talk about why it will help shift you from a place of anxiety to one of openness and love. Loving-kindness practice has been taught by spiritual teachers in different ways since the Buddha delivered his sermon twenty-six hundred years ago. The point of the practice, regardless of who is teaching it and how they do so, is to cultivate and reside in the love that already exists inside of you.

In English (my native tongue), the word "love" is tricky because it means I only have one word to express how I feel about the woman I hopefully will spend the rest of my life with and tacos: I love them both. Sanskrit has ninety-six words for love, Persian eighty. And while I can continue to quote bell hooks' excellent book on the topic, *All About Love*, I will say that what we are aiming for in loving-kindness meditation is a felt experience of loving in a free and dynamic manner. At the end of a session, you might have every image and aspirational phrase drop away and just experience a sense of openness and love and *boom!* That's it. Bonus: in this moment of complete openness? No anxiety.

The way many people in the West currently practice loving-kindness came about in the fifth century. An Indian Theravada Buddhist teacher known as Acariya Buddhaghosa received the Karaniya Metta Sutta from elders who received it from elders who received it from elders going back to the time the teachings were originally offered. He then systematized these teachings of the Buddha into the formal practice we now regularly refer to as loving-kindness.

As the formal practice of loving-kindness moved from India to new lands, the progression of steps and specific terms used have changed. It's a bit of a long-standing game of telephone, but the original message is clear based on the words of the Buddha: we offer aspirational well-being for all kinds of people, including ourselves.

We will do this practice together in the next chapter, but a bit of a warning first: after thousands of years of people doing this practice around the world, it finds its way to us in the West and we're the ones who go, "Actually, this practice is really hard." I have many theories about our capitalistic culture and how it molds us into always wanting to become better or more than who we truly are, but for now, I'll just say, "I get it. You may not have been trained from a young age to love and accept yourself unconditionally." Still, I encourage you to try this practice by starting with a contemplation of yourself.

As a warm-up, you can do an on-the-spot loving-kindness practice as you go about your day. One of my mentors, Sharon Salzberg, once shared how you can offer loving-kindness to yourself as an antidote to anxiety. You begin by chanting "May I be free from harm. May I be strong and healthy. May I be happy. May I live a life filled with ease," before moving on to extend those same wishes to the people you love and to the wider world. The whole process can take just a few minutes. She wrote, "When you say those wishes sincerely, every element of the practice is a relief. The phrases channel the energy [of anxiety] instead of allowing it to proliferate. As you do this, you are back in charge and you can feel the body relaxing as the space around your anxiety opens up and releases."[33]

In the formal loving-kindness meditation, we start with ourselves but then contemplate people we find it's easy to open our heart to. In some traditions, we start with a mentor or benefactor and then move into a close friend. I have studied with teachers who, knowing you may not have a benefactor who pays for your lodging and meals, lump these two together into "the person you really like." The sequence thereafter is pretty straightforward: we contemplate someone we don't know very well, a difficult person, and then we have an opportunity to break down the barriers by thinking of everyone thus far (you, your loved one, the "I don't know you" person, and this jerk) and then we radiate love to all beings.

People We Like

I am guessing you have some people in your life who you like; this is not a foreign concept. These are your family members, friends, people you date or are in long-term partnerships with, even puppies. (Yes, we don't have to limit loving-kindness practice just to people. If the people in your family are pissing you off, you can contemplate the family dog. I recently learned that my own wife, who is the person I often think of in this stage, does not contemplate me but our puppy instead.) The idea of, early on in your practice, bringing to mind someone you really like is that it's a good warm-up for your heart; it's easier to contemplate and offer love to your grandmother who always fed you sweets than the jerk at work. While my list above is not exhaustive, these are the people in your life who have shown you real kindness and support in the past.

People We Dislike

In our current society, it is easy to jump into polarities such as my side of the political aisle is made up of good people and the other side of the aisle is made up of monsters. It is hard for us to consider the humanity of these people we often villainize. Maybe you really dislike the current president or their closest advisors, or your local representative, or the latest person who decided to buy a gun and use it on innocents. I understand. But loving-kindness practice asks us to not write these people off and instead to consider their humanity.

People We Don't Know

Depending on who you are, you likely have one small group of people you like, and another small group of people you dislike, but then there's this gigantic group out there which we might label, "Who?" These are the people we don't know: our neighbors down the hall or the refugees being torn from family members at the border. It's the person who sat next to you on the subway, the construction worker making all that damn noise, earthquake survivors in a country you've never been to, and a celebrity who is on the cover of a magazine. There are so many of these people, all of whom are suffering in ways small or large. We can move from our current place of anxiety to one of openness simply by contemplating someone we like, dislike, or even don't know, and practicing loving-kindness for them.

The Phrases

When I first started practicing in the Tibetan Buddhist system, I was given some variation of the phrase "May you enjoy happiness and be free from suffering" for this practice. Maybe you love this phrase; if so, use it. It didn't resonate with me.

Years later, when I began studying with Theravada Buddhist and Insight Meditation Society teachers, I would hear phrases like,

"May you be happy," "May you be healthy," "May you feel safe," and "May you live with ease." Those really hit home.

Other variations like "May you feel peaceful" or my personal favorite, "May you feel loved" resonate deeply with me. Truth be told, I don't know if I first heard this last one from another teacher or it was an aspiration which arose from my own practice, and that's okay. Again, the point isn't to wish specific things for people like "May you get a new car" but to wish for their well-being and emanate love to them. Whatever phrases feel right to you are good ones to work with. Here's some more:

May I feel free
May I be well
May I be inspired
May I be free from fear
May I awaken
May I feel joy
May I be healed
May I be liberated

As you can tell, this is wishing an attitude of goodwill; we can wish ourselves and other people well, but the caveat here is that true happiness is something which ultimately each of us will have to discover for ourselves. Simply because we hope this person feels happy does not make us responsible for their happiness.

Knowing that we can't take responsibility for other people's happiness can be heartbreaking. I remember a time when I led loving-kindness practice at a homeless aide organization. Ten or so queer youth between the ages of sixteen and twenty-two sat in a circle and after I finished leading the practice, one of them raised their hands. "I don't have a question," they said, "but I spend a lot of time wishing for my own safety in the shelters." They went on to explain how they forget sometimes so many others in the room were doing the same thing. While I was chatting with this person afterward, they told me this practice made them feel not so alone. I kept a supportive face, but inwardly, my heart was breaking for them. There are so many people out there who have different lives than what we are familiar with, but we are not alone in wanting these very basic things.

The Benefits

The benefits of loving-kindness practice may be readily apparent by now: we become more open-hearted individuals and live a life marked by love, not anxiety or fear. This is the most transformative shift I have experienced. Yet, there is a traditional list the Buddha offered in the Discourse on the Benefits of Loving-Kindness (Metta Nisamsa Sutta). It is said if you do this practice:

» *You will sleep and wake more easily, plus have pleasant dreams.* Sounds good, right?
» *People will love you.* As my dearly departed nana used to say, "And why not?" Why wouldn't people love you if you are actively cultivating love right back?
» *Devas [spiritual beings] and animals will love you and devas will protect you.* Maybe you aren't into the idea of unseen beings—I understand. But who doesn't want to be the person at the party that the dog really wants to hang out with?
» *External dangers will not harm you.* While this is a precise translation, please don't run out into the streets after

practice and throw yourself into traffic.

» *Your face will be radiant.* Think of the money you will save on skin care products (I kid).

» *Your mind will be serene and you will die unconfused, and be reborn in happy realms.* Here we have the most important element: we internalize peace and live it over the course of our lives. If you believe in rebirth, this also ensures you have a favorable one and if you don't, at least you will have lived a meaningful life.[34]

In the next chapter, I will offer you the full, step-by-step guidance for how to practice loving-kindness so that you can begin to wake up the heart to those people you like, dislike, and those many beings you don't yet know.*

* You can find a recording of this meditation at lodrorinzler.com/anxiety.

CHAPTER 16

An Introduction to Loving-Kindness Meditation

Perhaps everything terrible is in its deepest being something that needs our love.

—Rainer Maria Rilke

Begin by taking the meditation posture discussed during the shamatha instruction—uplifted but relaxed. Take three to five minutes to settle your mind through mindfulness of the breath practice.

Now bring to mind an image of yourself. It could be you as you last saw yourself in the mirror, or you in your favorite outfit, or (if you suspect you might have a hard time offering loving-kindness to yourself) you as a young child, perhaps seven or eight years old. Make it visceral, almost like you're sitting down across the table from yourself. Let your heart soften. Holding this image in mind, make these aspirational phrases, pausing after each one to let it sink in:

May I be happy.
May I be healthy.
May I feel safe.
May I feel loved.

Along the way, a felt sense of what it might mean to experience any of these things may arise; this is totally fine. Just acknowledge it and continue on to the next phrase. If big stories come up like "Well I'd feel safe if my boss wasn't so demanding," just acknowledge the thought and move onto the next phrase. Repeat this set of phrases three times. Let the image dissolve. Take a breath.

Now bring to mind an image of someone you really love and admire. It could be a family member, romantic partner, or even a close friend or mentor. Make this image visceral as well—you can think about the way they do their hair, the way they smile, or the way they normally dress. Once this image is vivid, let your heart soften. Holding this image in mind, make these aspirational phrases, pausing after each one to let it sink in:

May you be happy.
May you be healthy.
May you feel safe.
May you feel loved.

If you prefer to use their name ("May Dave be happy" or "May Nancy be happy") that's fine. Similar to before, certain notions may arise and it is okay; continue on with the practice. Repeat this set of phrases three times. Let the image dissolve. Take a breath.

Now bring to mind an image of someone you don't know very well. Perhaps this is someone who you see during your morning commute, or who lives in your neighborhood, or you saw on the news. You can think of where you saw them and the way they looked on the given day. Just like the people we know much better, this person deserves these basic qualities in their life. Consider their humanity for a moment and offer these same aspirations for them:

May you be happy.
May you be healthy.
May you feel safe.
May you feel loved.

Repeat this set of phrases three times. Let the image dissolve. Take a breath.

Now bring to mind an image of someone you are currently having a hard time with. This should not be the most difficult person in your life at this point, or anyone who has caused you deep pain, but someone you are currently butting heads with. It may help to imagine this person sitting down in a relaxed posture, smiling lightly (i.e., not on the attack). Even if we are having a hard time with them right now, we can't disregard the fact that they are suffering. In fact, if they weren't suffering so much, we likely wouldn't be in conflict with them. Consider their humanity for a moment and offer these same aspirations to the best of your ability:

May you be happy.
May you be healthy.
May you feel safe.

May you feel loved.

Repeat this set of phrases three times. Let the image dissolve. Take a breath.

Now bring to mind all of the beings you have contemplated thus far: yourself, your loved one, the person you don't know very well, and this difficult person. They can be hanging out in space or in an imagined living room—this is very much up to you. At this point, we are dissolving the boundaries of opinion around them. It's not "I like you" and "I don't like you" or "me versus you." It's us. While holding this group of beings in mind, offer these aspirations:

May we be happy.
May we be healthy.
May we feel safe.
May we feel loved.

Repeat this set of phrases three times. Let the image dissolve. Take a breath.

Begin to let your love radiate through all the pores of your body. Contemplate the people who live on your block or in your city or town. Offer these phrases for them. Expand out to contemplate the people who live in your state or province. Offer these phrases for them. Take your time as you continue to zoom out to your country and beyond. Make the aspiration:

May all beings be happy.
May all beings be healthy.
May all beings feel safe.

May all beings feel loved.

Let the words and images fall away. Notice how you are feeling—any sense of openness, appreciation or love. Whatever you are experiencing is fine, just notice. Let yourself remain there.

CHAPTER 17

Building a Compassionate Society

Promise me I'll be happy.

—Charlie

I can't promise you that. I can promise you won't be alone.

—Nadia, *Russian Doll*

When I find myself lost in anxiety, I reflect on how I am simultaneously offered countless opportunities for compassion. While I write this chapter, I am in fact bombarded by construction noises from outside. The on-again, off-again screech of the saw blade hits me and my shoulders shoot right up to my ears each time in response. Yet, I have a choice here: I could get annoyed at these beings who are "ruining" my rare writing time or I could consider that the men and women outside are just doing their job, thereby developing compassion for them.

The construction workers have families and people they love and who love them, just like me. They have financial problems and worry about getting by sometimes, just like me. They have anxiety and work-stressors and all sorts of things I may never know about, but I can assume that they long to be happy, healthy, safe, and loved—just like me. Simply by contemplating these people I don't necessarily know—for minutes here and there—humanizes them and brings me from a place of anxiety to one of compassion and a deeper connection to those around me.

The second of the Four Immeasurables, compassion, is simply us opening our heart in the face of suffering. When you're confronted with stressful situations, it is immensely helpful to touch in with your heart and open up to a wider possibility of connection. Let's say you're walking down the hallway at work, lost in your stress about deadlines. But you've been meditating, so you actually catch yourself doing it! In this moment, you could go back to your anxiety or you can raise your gaze and see where you might be able to find a moment of compassion.

As if on cue, the coworker you are friends with appears, clearly getting chewed out by her boss. Instead of being lost in thought, you offer a phrase of support, "May you be free of your pain and sorrow" or "May you find peace" either in your mind or at the volume just below a whisper, so only you can hear. In that moment, you feel connected instead of drained. It's simple, yet remarkably effective. You don't have to go about muttering aspirational phrases under your breath, of course. Even just pausing long enough to let the suffering of this other person touch your heart will help steer you to more compassionate activity long-term.

If this sounds quite hard, let's start by offering compassion to ourselves.

Compassion for Yourself

When you meditate, you realize that it's okay to look directly at yourself—to become familiar with who you are—and that who you are is okay in this very moment. And yes, sometimes you experience pain or confusion when you look directly at yourself. I won't deny that. Yet, as angel Kyodo williams Sensei once wrote, "The thing about our pain and our suffering is that until it is met and seen for what it is, it doesn't go anywhere."[35] When we lean into looking at our pain, we begin to heal and to accept the totality of who we are. One way of doing this work comes from Thich Nhat Hanh: we can simply pause either during our meditation, or when we feel particularly stuck in anxiety, we can say, "May I learn to look at myself with the eyes of understanding and compassion."[36]

Just because you might consider yourself a messy human being, it doesn't mean you need fixing. You just need to look at yourself with the eyes of understanding and compassion. You don't need anything external to make you more lovable. You are inherently lovable. Just as you are. You just need to discover this simple truth. When we're mentally flailing we can say Thich Nhat Hanh's words, which are a nice way of saying, "I see you, dear friend. You are suffering." We can be with our suffering without the pressure of having to fix ourselves. We can know it will pass and, in the meantime, hang out with it.

The more we practice looking at the core of who we are, our basic goodness, the more we breed resilience and resourcefulness so that we can offer compassion to others. As the Dalai Lama once said, "If you do not have the capacity to love yourself, then there is simply no basis on which to build a sense of caring toward others."[37]

Compassion for Others

At the top of the chapter, I quote a poignant moment from the Netflix series *Russian Doll*. One of our leads, Charlie, poised to jump to his death, stands at the top of a building. Despondently, he turns to our heroine, Nadia, and demands, "Promise me I'll be happy." Nadia replies with brutal honesty: "I can't promise you that. I can promise you won't be alone." The notion of compassion is that we begin to glimpse the humanity and suffering of those around us and our heart naturally blossoms, empathizing with their pain. We may not be able to suddenly heal their difficulties but we can be open-heartedly there for them. With so many of us feeling despair and loneliness these days, to bear witness to the pain of another is a true gift of support.

Throughout this book, I have used a particular term: meditation practice. When I use the term "meditation practice," I am acknowledging exactly that: when you sit and tune into a sense of presence and kindness, you are practicing to offer mindfulness and compassion in the rest of your life. Thich Nhat Hanh once said, "To love someone, you need to be there for them 100 percent. The mantra 'I am here for you' says that I care about you, I enjoy being in your presence. It helps the other person to feel supported and happy."[38]

When you are present and open to the suffering of another person, not only compassion dawns but also skillful action. Thanks to your consistent mindfulness practice, you are in touch with reality enough to see how best to help the people around you.

When I was in my twenties, I founded a nonprofit called the Institute for Compassionate Leadership, which brought together meditation principles, community-organizing skills, and practical leadership know-how to form a six-month part-time training meant to produce more mindful and open-hearted leaders in the world around us.[39]

The founding principle was straightforward enough: anyone can be a leader. A leader is not necessarily "the boss" or "the breadwinner," it could be anyone who, when asked to step up in the present moment and serve, does so. This concept implies that you can serve as a leader whenever you are walking by some stairs and see a woman trying to navigate her kid and their stroller. It's in the moment that you offer to help get them up the stairs. It means that you can serve as a leader when a colleague is having a hard time meeting a deadline and you pitch in alongside them to make sure everything gets done. It can look like you seeing someone drop trash into the street and grabbing it and disposing of it properly.

None of the examples I just gave about leadership are particularly sexy. No one is going to give you a raise or write about your good qualities in the *New York Times* because of them. But, in that moment, you are showing up in a way that nudges our society in the right direction, thus serving as the leader this world needs.

My definition of compassionate leadership includes anyone who steps up in a given situation, as long as they are moved by the aspiration to be of benefit to the people they are working with. Because we are training to be more present, we can see what other people need from us. We are not forcing our fixed idea of how to be helpful on other people whom we pity. We are showing up alongside them, shoulder-to-shoulder, and asking, "How can I help you?" In this way, we come at leadership from a place of empathy, knowing how other people are suffering in similar core ways that we do, acknowledging our shared experience and humanity.

Compassion for Society

At the time of this writing, there is incredible fear and panic on a global level. A virus is sweeping the world that is leading to a great number of deaths, we have volatile economies, we have various states of emergency, and the media keeps coming up with new ways to highlight the violence and upset of this epidemic. Three months ago, the main concern for many people I know was the vast political divide in the United States and the recurring deep, ecological disasters. Three months from now, who knows?

If you recall from previous chapters, society may often appear as one big thing "out there" but we are constantly cocreating it with the people around us. The increased level of fear and anxiety that exists on a societal level starts with people like you and me working with (or not working with) our own minds.

There is a Sanskrit term, *bodhisattva*. As you know, *bodhi* can be translated as "open" or "awake" while *sattva* can be "being" or "warrior." In this case, the term warrior isn't someone who goes out and fights other people but instead is a person who is willing to go to war with their own neurosis in order to wake up for the benefit of those around them.

Everyone should strive to be a bodhisattva, an open-hearted warrior of compassion. As Pema Chödrön once said, "The world needs people who are trained like this—bodhisattva politicians, bodhisattva police, bodhisattva parents, bodhisattva bus drivers, bodhisattvas at the bank and at the grocery store. In all levels of society we are needed. We are needed to transform our minds and actions for the sake of other people and for the future of the world."[40]

I am making a big ask when I propose softening your heart to include the pain and suffering of the world around you. When

I get disheartened about how best to show up and help society, I think of something else Chögyam Trungpa Rinpoche supposedly said when asked about the complex notion of karma: "Everything is predetermined . . . until now." In other words, we have the habitual, sometimes negative way we have always done things and this feeds into the habitual way that society has plodded along to this point, which has gotten us to where we are now.

Then, we have now. Now, in this moment, you have a choice. You can lay low and be self-absorbed, continuing to perpetuate old habits around anxiety and hope somehow the world will fix itself (it won't). Alternatively, you can try something new. In this moment, right now, you can show up compassionately for the people in your life, in your small societies, and see how doing so might shift the dynamic in those communities. The more you feed your own mindfulness and compassion into those societies— be it your work society, your family, your relationship, your gym, anything really—the more those principles will naturally ripple out and affect society overall.

I need to acknowledge that the compassionate leader does not operate alone. You can ask for support from others. You can engage the people in your life, including the people you like, those you don't, and even those you don't (yet) know in compassionate dialogue, by inviting them into conversation, specifically the types of conversations you may not normally have. If you need support from them, you ask for it. If they ask support from you, you offer it to the best of your ability.

The beauty of having launched a meditation practice is that you can appreciate the potency of now. Now, in the present moment, anything is possible. You can show up for whoever is right in front of you and apply your mindfulness to really see how to be of benefit. Yes, there is great uncertainty out there but you know this does not give you the right to turn your back on others; you can recognize the basic goodness in everyone you meet and offer an open heart, without attachment.

CHAPTER 18

Exchanging Oneself for Others

There is a place where giving and receiving love becomes indistinguishable, where you, me, and us blend. That place is reached when you stop imagining that love is a feeling and begin to think of it as a gesture or a way of holding your mind.

—Susan Piver, *The Four Noble Truths of Love* [41]

Another tool we can add to our working-with-anxiety tool belt is *tonglen* practice. Tonglen is a Tibetan word which can be translated as "sending and receiving." In tonglen, we learn to consider other people and what they may be going through. On the in-breath, we breathe in the things we believe to be painful or uncomfortable for others and breathe out, sending those people pleasing, soothing qualities. If you're a parent, this is a practice you can do when you are anxious about your child. If you're in a relationship and your loved one is suffering, this is a practice you can do instead of fretting over them. There are so many opportunities for us to engage this beautiful practice, moving us from a place of focusing solely on our pain to opening our hearts to those around us.

We start with our own textured feelings of suffering, then consider someone we know, an interpersonal relationship, and ultimately end up making our practice large enough to include all beings who are going through what they are going through on a societal level.*

Start by engaging in shamatha for five to ten minutes. Afterward, raise your gaze. Relax your mind for a moment. Let there be a gap with no object for your attention. Simply rest.

Now transition to not only experiencing your breath but also allowing various textures to ride each wave of it. As you breathe in, imagine you are inhaling hot and heavy air. As you breathe out, imagine you are exhaling cool, fresh, and light air. Continue with this pattern, breathing in heaviness and breathing out lightness, until it is familiar to you. The heaviness may feel like a sense of suffering; the lightness, a sense of well-being.

You can even get bigger with this practice, imagining you are breathing through all the pores of your body. On the in-breath, heavy, hot air enters every pore. On the out-breath, coolness flows from every pore.

Having worked with the experience of texture in this practice for a few minutes, bring to mind a loved one who is having a hard time. As you picture them, you can imagine the clothes they normally wear or the details of their face to make it quite vivid.

As you breathe in, imagine you are breathing in their pain. For example, if you have a friend who is suffering from cancer,

---

* You can find a recording of this meditation at lodrorinzler.com/anxiety.

you might understand how they feel weak, claustrophobic, or angry. Imagine breathing those sensations in. You are not, of course, literally absorbing anyone's disease or heartbreak. This is a visualization. But, you are empathizing with their experience.

As you breathe out, send out with the breath a sense of calm, strength, relief, or spaciousness to this person. Whatever comfort you can offer in this moment, offer it as you exhale. In: their fear, confusion, pain. Out: joy, happiness, safety.

After a few minutes of this, we go even further, extending the practice larger than just one person. Bring to mind everyone who is going through this type of suffering. If it is a transgender person who is lonely or scared, you can consider all transgender people who may feel this way, then all beings who are experiencing loneliness and fear. If it is someone who recently lost a loved one and is experiencing grief or anxiety, you can consider everyone who may have lost a loved one and feel a similar way. You extend your sense of ease and bravery to them all. Here, you can make this practice radiate far and wide so every single being out there feels a sense of comfort as a result.

To conclude, return to shamatha for a few minutes. Ground yourself back in your body through your focus on the breath, letting it return you to the earthiness of the present moment.

CHAPTER 19

Cultivating Sympathetic Joy

*We create most of our suffering, so it should be logical that
we also have the ability to create more joy.*

—His Holiness the Dalai Lama[42]

Want to feel like a loser? Compare yourself to others.

At least, this is what I was told early on as a student of Buddhism.
In my case, the teacher in question was trying to tell me that if I sat
in meditation and compared myself to what I thought other people
were experiencing, then I would be sorely misguided and believe
I was failing at it. In fact, what I thought was a group of people
resting peacefully in the nature of their own minds were actually a
bunch of fidgety, anxious people with a torrent of thoughts running
through their heads—just like me. Somehow, knowing that we all
struggle in some way with the practice (and in life) helped me so
that I didn't feel so bad about my experience.

This advice about comparing mind can be applied to any
number of things. Too often when we compare ourselves to others,

we focus less on what we do have and notice only the things we do not, leading to self-induced anxiety.

Your career could be going well, for example, but you turn your attention to how everyone else you know seems to be in a happy relationship right now. A minute into such a train of thought and you're stressed about how you'll never get married. Or you are happily married but when you visit with friends, you get disheartened because they have a nicer home than you and spend your time with them thinking about how your finances aren't where you want them to be. Or you have a comfy living situation, but you see Facebook photos of your friend on a beach and suddenly get a hit that you work harder and take less time for yourself than just about anyone you know. The moment you start single-mindedly focusing on what you don't have is the moment you spiral down a seemingly endless rabbit hole of stress and despair.

Comparing mind can derail your open-heartedness. Thich Nhat Hanh employs the analogy of pouring a handful of salt into a cup of water. If we do so, it becomes undrinkable. If we pour a handful of salt into a river, people can continue to draw from it and enjoy it. This is because the river is immense. In the same way, he says, "When our hearts are small, our understanding and compassion are limited, and we suffer . . . But when our hearts expand, these same things don't make us suffer anymore."[43]

In order to make our heart as vast as a river, we can cultivate the third form of love, *mudita*. Mudita is another Sanskrit word that is generally translated as "sympathetic joy" or "altruistic joy." If compassion is us opening our heart in the face of the suffering we see in others, mudita is us opening our heart in the face of their happiness. When we get stuck in our own negative thought patterns, we could practice sympathetic joy by shifting from focusing on our failures to a form of love which acknowledges and rejoices in the joy of the people around us.

Meditation for Increasing Sympathetic Joy

If you find yourself a victim of comparing mind, stop what you are doing. Come into your body. Take three deep breaths in through the nose then out through the mouth. Notice the weight of your body on the earth beneath you. Transition into experiencing the natural cycle of your breathing.

Now, raise your gaze. If you are in a space with other people, look about and acknowledge them, regardless of whether you know them or not. If you are alone, bring to mind various people in your life—those you love, those you don't know very well and, if you would like, even those you have a hard time with. Now, see if you can rejoice in someone else's happiness.

In this moment, it may not be advisable to turn your attention to the person you are typically jealous of. Perhaps instead it's an older couple sitting hand-in-hand near you on the subway or young children playing down the street or, if you really struggle with comparing mind and those two things remind you that you may never meet someone or have kids, see if you can notice or bring to mind a puppy and notice how happy they are. Simply take a few minutes to notice the joy in those around you.

If you would like, you could even bring to mind people in your life—friends, family, loved ones—who have things to celebrate such as a new job or baby. In either of these cases, you can voice the aspiration "May your happiness and good fortune continue" or "May your happiness not diminish."

When you are ready, re-engage with other people. You can start conversations with or call those you know and inquire about their recent good news, celebrating and magnifying their success. Here, we are looking for ways to rejoice in the happiness of others, even if it's the smallest of details in their life. When we do, we end up experiencing joy ourselves and they feel supported and loved.

The more we celebrate the success of others, the more we might be inspired to look at our own successes in a new light. Instead of anxiously longing to meet a mythical Prince(ss) Charming, we relish the fact that we get to do the work that we do. Instead of being jealous because we don't have a Pinterest-worthy home, we celebrate our partner, knowing that home is where the heart is. Instead of being frustrated and stressed about how much we work, we learn to enjoy our downtime with friends and family. Overall, the more we magnify and rejoice in the joy of others while celebrating the little things in our own life, the more likely we see happiness in the world and smile, knowing everyone around us is—again—just like me.

CHAPTER 20

The Thing We All Want: Equanimity

We can't have an enlightened society or a sane and peaceful world if the individuals within it are stuck in small, fixed mind.

—Pema Chödrön, *Welcoming the Unwelcome* [44]

As Sharon Salzberg wrote, "Equanimity endows lovingkindness, compassion, and sympathetic joy with their sense of patience, that ability to be constant and to endure, even if the love, sympathy, or rejoicing is unreturned, even through all their ups and downs."[45] When I say the word equanimity you might think, "Yes please." The Sanskrit word upeksha is commonly translated as "equanimity" but it's not just about feeling even-keeled; it's a bit more expansive than such a definition. In fact, I prefer Thich Nhat Hanh's translation, which is "inclusiveness." Inclusiveness means we can open our heart wide and embrace everyone we encounter as a recipient of our love. He once said on this topic, "When you love one person, it's an opportunity for you to love everyone, all beings."[46]

Sometimes when I feel overwhelmed by my own anxiety I like to go for a walk. I'm not much of a hiker, although I understand the appeal. I often just walk around my neighborhood, at night when it's not very crowded, and make it a practice in equanimity. The practice is quite straightforward: as I encounter people, I let go of the stories about my own issues and simply smile at them, opening my heart to them.

As I do, I may encounter someone friendly who is walking their dog and my impulse is to like them. I might see someone talking loudly on their cell phone and find myself disliking them (but smiling anyway). I may be surrounded by people I don't know. But the point of the practice is to transcend the "I like/dislike/ignore" tendency because all of them are inherently worthy of my love.

His Holiness the 17th Karmapa, Ogyen Trinley Dorje, is the head of the Kagyu school of Tibetan Buddhism. He once said,

> I want to share with you a feeling I have. I feel
> that my love does not have to remain within the
> limitations of my own life or body. I imagine that if
> I am no longer in the world, my love could still be
> present. I want to place my love on the moon and
> let the moon hold my love. Let the moon be the
> keeper of my love, offering it to everyone just as the
> moon sends its light to embrace the whole earth.[47]

This vast form of love may seem crazy to you. Yet, so much of our internal suffering spawns from the belief that there are people who we should like and people we don't. The former should only shower us with praise and love and the latter are always waiting in ambush to strike us down. This is simply not the case. Everyone is suffering. We are all doing the best we can. We all possess basic goodness—and we all have times we act from a confused state. In order to show up and help the world around us, we have to move from a (as Pema Chödrön puts it at the top of this chapter) small, fixed mind into a mind which is inclusive of everyone.

When you encounter people acting from a confused state, your habitual tendency may be to close off your heart and tell yourself lots of stories about how they are a bad person, filling the mind with anxiety. It is hard to fight that tendency and open your heart to them. When you find yourself lost in those stories, pause. Take a breath.

Feel your body—slowly scan for any tension you're holding starting at the base of the feet up through the top of your skull, relaxing any tight muscles along the way.

Take a moment to experience your body breathing.

Now bring to mind someone you are having a hard time with right now. You can imagine them sitting in a relaxed posture, i.e., not on the attack. Notice any tendency to shut your heart down and see if you can remain open to their presence. Offer them an aspirational phrase of well-being. You could use one I mentioned in the loving-kindness section, but some common phrases for equanimity practice are:

I wish you happiness but cannot make your choices for you.
I will care for you but cannot keep you from suffering.
May we all accept things as they are.

If one of these phrases resonates, say it slowly three times, pausing between each recitation for the words to truly land in your being. When you're ready, take another deep breath and reenter your day.

When we do this type of practice, we realize we cannot control other people. They may continue to suffer and continue to lash out at those around them because they are suffering. All we can do is aspire that they wake up their own mind and heart so they realize a sense of happiness. We can be open and patient with them through all their ups and downs.

There is something so beautiful about equanimity. When I think of equanimity, the image I often reflect on is a mountain. When the strong winds hit a mountain, they are rebuffed but the mountain remains unchanged. Yet, if these strong winds encounter a wilted flower, they can pull the flower up from the ground and whip it around. When the strong winds of life come your way, would you rather be the mountain or the flower?

When you sit in meditation, you emulate the mountain. You have the strong base, which your body rooted into the ground. Then you lift up through your spine and your head is the peak. Whatever thoughts arise in your practice, you remain unmoved; you acknowledge them and return to the breath. As you continue to engage in shamatha and the Four Immeasurable practices, you are learning to be mountain-like. You are learning to cultivate the patience to endure the good times and the bad that life throws at you, remaining stable, grounded, and strong.

The Four Immeasurables—loving-kindness, compassion, sympathetic joy, and equanimity—show us how even when people stress us out or we get lost in our anxiety, we have a choice: we can turn inward and lose ourselves in our negative patterns or we can raise our gaze and see how we can offer love, seeing our way through the stressful situation from a place of clarity. The choice is ours, and the love option gets easier the more we choose it.

PART THREE

From Anxiety To Compassionate Activity

CHAPTER 21

Nothing (Including Anxiety) Is As Real As We Think

Regard all dharmas as dreams.

—Atisha Dipamkara Shrijnana[48]

Thus far, you might be following along thinking, "Okay, I'll meditate to help with my anxiety. This bodhichitta stuff is interesting and maybe I'll give the loving-kindness thing a try too." Then you hit this chapter and perhaps put the book down for a week. WTF does "Regard all dharmas as dreams" have to do with your anxiety? Good question. In short, everything. We will now build on the teachings on love from the previous section by adding in the Buddhist special sauce: the teachings on emptiness.

Let's start back in the eleventh century. Atisha Dipamkara Shrijnana was an amazing teacher in the Kadampa school of Tibetan Buddhism. He is widely credited as systematizing what is known as *lojong. Lo* can be translated from Tibetan as "mind" and *jong* as "training." In other words, he took the essence of Buddhism and made it accessible for people by condensing the teachings into fifty-nine pithy mind-training slogans. Prior to Atisha, this particular set of teachings were held closely to the chest by the monastic community, but he saw how relevant they were to lay practitioners and made them available to the world at-large.

In this section, we will look at ten of the slogans and relate them back to how we can understand things as they are and, as a result, let go of anxiety and move to a place of freedom and open-heartedness. The slogans address two key concepts: absolute and relative bodhichitta. "Absolute" is a term that invites us to look at the very nature of reality itself, seeing through our confusion and placing us in an open and relaxed state (hence the freedom). "Relative" bodhichitta is the experience of us bringing this perspective into our day-to-day activity in a compassionate and caring way (hence the open-heartedness).

Circling back then, what does "Regard all dharmas as dreams" even mean? "Dharma," when singular, can refer to the teachings of the Buddha, but when it is plural, it refers to all phenomena. So Atisha is asking us to regard whatever we encounter in the world around us as lightly as we would a dream. He is pointing out how we take ourselves and our world so seriously—and we don't have to do that. It's eleventh-century slang for "Let that shit go," but with a twist.

The twist on viewing our world as dreamlike is related to the Buddhist teachings on emptiness. In the first section of this book, I explored emptiness of self: how our ego holds us back from relaxing with things as they are. Here, we look at how it's not just us, it's how everything else is empty of solid, permanent, constant nature too.

We are not as solid and fixed as we might suspect. Science has proven that our entire body undergoes a process wherein every cell dies and is replaced over a period of seven years. That means this body that we think of as one continuous thing? Constantly new!

It's not just our body; our emotions and thoughts are ephemeral and ever-changing as well. If I asked you what you were anxious about this time one year ago to the day, you likely couldn't tell me the specifics because that story and its related emotional upheaval you were clinging to so tightly changed over time. The more we look at ourselves, the more we realize how every aspect of who we think we are is empty of permanent, fixed nature. Even our anxiety—this albatross around our neck—is not as solid and real as we think.

Having considered emptiness of self, now we can look at emptiness of other. Everything around us lacks a fixed, permanent state of being, just like us. When we look at the circumstances of our life, it's impossible to pin one thing down and say "This part never changes." This is because everything is in flux. The seasons change. Our loved ones age. Even our cherished possessions come together and fall apart over time. If everything lacks a lasting, permanent nature then, Atisha argues, shouldn't we treat our world as more ephemeral and fluid, not taking it so seriously?

This is a nice idea, but it's also something we can experience in our meditation practice. As Pema Chödrön once wrote, "You can experience this open, un-fixated quality in sitting meditation; all that arises in your mind—hate love and all the rest—is not solid. Although the experience can get extremely vivid, it is just a product of your mind. Nothing solid is really happening."[49] When we consider that our strong emotions (including fear, anxiety, or worry) are just products of our mind, we realize we can relax around them.

Anxiety and other stuck parts of ourselves can be confronted by simply realizing they are not as solid and real as we might suspect (they are empty of permanent nature) and this frees us up to be very kind to ourselves and others (offering our bodhichitta).

When we become aware of this perspective, the strong emotions become less scary. They come knocking on your door and you see them for what they are. You don't run and hide in the other room. Instead you say, "Oh, you again!" and invite them in for tea. Anxiety and fear may not be your favorite guests, but you can at least have a sense of humor about how often they pop by, knowing that once they are done with tea, they will go along their merry way.

This view, how you regard whatever you encounter—including your stressful triggers—as dreamlike, as not so permanent nor solid, signals a fundamental switch in how you normally operate. Instead of clinging to fear, anxiety, or whatever emotions that come knocking, you're tuning into reality as it is in the present moment and relaxing into it. You are confident that your emotions will come and go. They can move through you. You don't have to struggle or get too attached to them but instead know them to be ephemeral, and relax back into the present moment.

CHAPTER 22

Compassion in a Dumpster Fire

When the world is filled with evil, transform all mishaps into the path of bodhi.

—Atisha Dipamkara Shrijnana

Sometimes it feels like the world is on fire and there is nothing we can do about it. When things are falling apart in your personal life, or your relationships are chaotic, or you are getting nonstop news alerts about the current global calamity, it's often the time when you want to shut down your heart and mind, climb into bed, and hide out. I get it. I truly do.

Then along comes our friend Atisha, suggesting that for some reason this is *the* moment for you to wake up your heart and mind by looking at whatever's on fire as part of your spiritual path. He whispers our next slogan in your ear: "When the world is filled with evil, transform all mishaps into the path of bodhi." To recap, "bodhi" can be translated as open or awake, so Atisha is offering the very advanced point of view that whatever we find wrong in the world can be transmuted as fuel for compassionately waking up to reality as it is.

The way this works is we don't merely react to whatever we perceive as evil. As I mentioned before, I am writing this chapter during what I imagine will be a historic time: the coronavirus pandemic of 2020. There was an interesting moment when, after many countries went into quarantine, a number of college students decided to keep their spring break plans in Florida. There was a viral video that surfaced of these young people (Good Lord, I'm old, using that term) speaking to reporters about how they weren't going to let this pandemic ruin their vacation.

Oh, the clap back! I had never seen the Internet so united in coming down on a given group. In this case, some people even labeled these partiers "evil." The fixed opinion was that everyone else was sacrificing deeply to prevent further spread of the virus and these kids were potentially spreading it everywhere. When we think of politics, there are a number of people on one side of the aisle and many on the other and it's somewhere near 50/50. In this case, we had a group of naive college kids trying to enjoy themselves and 99.9% of the world said, "How fucking dare you."

The core teaching offered in this case is to loosen the tight hold we have on this is "good," "bad," "for me," or "against me" and see things as they truly are. There are scared people, worried about their health and their loved ones. There are confused college students worried about missing out on life. The capital T truth is that everyone here is suffering in some way. To cling to the notion of good versus evil will only cause us more suffering.

When you have labeled an individual or a group as "evil," it is worth that considering your fixed opinion is likely blocking you from your own innate wakefulness. Thich Nhat Hanh offers the practice of asking "Are you sure?" to help move us away from a stuck point of view into one of deeper understanding. When something seemingly evil pops up in your life and stories emerge around why they are wrong and you are right, just ask yourself, "Are you sure?" Are you sure that this person is out to get you? Are you sure that this project failing spells the end of your career? Are you sure that text means your partner no longer cares for you?

When you get gently inquisitive with your experience, you can loosen the hold your anxiety and fear have on you and, in that moment, relax back into the present. You can come to your breath, your old friend, and allow it to anchor you in the here and now. By asking "Are you sure?" you let go of the fixed labels that keep you separated from yourself and others.

This particular slogan falls under a section of Atisha's work that focuses on patience. Especially if we are prone to anxiety, we often think of patience as something of a grin-and-bear-it situation: if we just wait long enough and don't freak out, then our circumstances will change. Granted, this is true, but the Buddhist notion of patience is a bit larger than this definition. Patience is not just waiting until you get to do what you want. It is relating fully with a situation, even if it is painful or scares the hell out of you.

The Buddhist notion of patience comes from not getting lost in those fixed expectations. You can drop your ideas of how things should be and open to the flow of how things will happen. You can think of patience as an act of being open to whatever comes your way, so it's less a "wait and see" affair but more a process of "being with" your experience.

Patience is easy to practice when you know something is going to happen eventually; it is far more difficult an asset when you don't know what's going to happen next. During the first few weeks of the global pandemic, most of my meditation students turned to me, assuming I possessed an infinite knowledge of virology and asked, "When do you think things will return to normal?" My answer, over and over again was "We don't know." I would go on to point out that instead of spending all of our mental energy being anxious about what might happen, we may need to learn to become comfortable with the idea of not knowing. When your personal life or the world overall appears to be filled with evil triggers, you might feel groundless and scared. You might fill your head with lots of stories about "What if . . . " and freak yourself out. But you don't know what will happen! Instead of meeting groundlessness with lots of stories about what might go wrong, you are being invited to ground down and open to the present moment.

Instead of getting lost in "what if," you are being invited into "right now." When you are able to enter this moment, you have a greater chance of seeing situations clearly, and responding in a way that is in line with what is actually going on as opposed to living based in your biased notions of how things should be.

You can even write the words "Are you sure?" on a Post-it note and stick it on the wall to remind yourself to reflect on whether the seemingly evil thing occurring is exactly what you think it is, or if you can open to new possibilities and respond from a place of openness.

When we respond to what we may normally perceive as "wrong" from a place of bodhi, we are waking up to life *as it is*. Not as we wish it would be: as it is. In Buddhism, we are constantly striving to understand what is going on in our own minds and the world around us. Remembering this slogan helps us get inquisitive and shift our view from doom and gloom to one of possibility. This slogan invites us to consider whatever is going on as part of our spiritual path.

One last note about this slogan: when we don't harden our hearts against the perceived evil in the world, we are cultivating hope for a better tomorrow. It can be hard to have hope at times. We live in such an anxious and stressed-out world with so much inequality that even mentioning this word "hope" may make you roll your eyes. I get it; it's hard not to get overwhelmed by the chaos and injustice in the world around us.

Sharon Salzberg once said, "Hope is often about how we want the world to be. As if life would be perfect if only you could get that thing, person, or experience. Or if the world were better in this or that way . . . One can get lost in this craving, which only increases separation from the world as it is."[50] Atisha's advice is that when things feel bad, don't put up walls between you and the world, wishing things to be another way. Lean into your experience and remain grounded and present to whatever emerges, not attached to a particular outcome.

You have faced adversity before. You have seen times when things felt chaotic and heavy and you are still here. There is hope in knowing you are strong and, having weathered past storms, you can weather this one.

Developing patience may not solve the multitude of problems in the world, but it will allow you to remain open and present enough to skillfully determine how to help move the needle in the right direction. What you perceive as bad or evil will continue to be a part of life, but you can face it with bodhichitta and see your way through. This is hope based in reality.

CHAPTER 23

Even Your Ex Deserves Your Gratitude

Be grateful to everyone.

—Atisha Dipamkara Shrijnana

In the first section of this book I explored how gratitude practices can move us from a place of focusing solely on our anxiety to a place of openness, realizing the abundance right under our noses. Often when I work with gratitude teachings, it's a way to move my attention from focusing on my suffering or what I do not have to placing my mental energy on experiencing appreciation, celebrating what I do.

In the next pithy slogan, Atisha asks us to take our gratitude practice a step further, instructing us to be grateful not just for the people in our life whom we like but for all beings. In fact, some teachers translate this slogan as "Contemplate the great kindness of everyone."

"Everyone" is a big ask though. Everyone includes your ex, the coworker you dislike, that politician who you believe is ruining the earth—everyone. We are being asked to look directly at some of the beings who may cause us stress and anxiety and find some aspect of them that we can appreciate, shifting our narrow perspective to a much larger one.

Traditionally this slogan "Be grateful to everyone" refers to how we could consider the difficult people in our life as worthy of our gratitude because they are helping us to become more spiritually grown up. The Tibetan Buddhist teacher Traleg Rinpoche once said, "We are only mature spiritually and psychologically when we are tested."[51] Every time we encounter an obstacle in relating to the difficult people in our life and work through it, we become that much more compassionate and resilient. Without the difficult person we would not have evolved in such a way, and for that we should be grateful to them.

Looking at the title of this chapter you may be thinking, "Hell no, Lodro. My ex is a dirty, cheating, piece of scum and I will never be grateful for him." While your ex may not have intended to show you kindness when he was trying to sleep with your best friend, we are looking at the situation through a new lens as a way to lessen the stress around it and move us to a place of contentment. In simpler terms, if we give up the ghost of resentment, we experience relief. In order to get there, we may need to consider the good that arises from what we consider "the bad."

Another way to consider gratitude for the jerks in your life is to contemplate their great suffering. Everyone is in pain in some way. Some people can't sit with their pain and, as a result, act out in ways that cause great harm to others. I have done so in the past. Have you? I imagine it's a possibility. Even acknowledging this helps us wake up our hearts to feel empathy for these people who are so clearly hurt and creating pain for others as a result of their suffering. As Pema Chödrön once wrote, "If we learn to open our hearts, anyone, including the people who drive us crazy, can be our teacher."

Gratitude Practice: Round 2

To build on the previous work we did in moving from anxiety to gratitude, try this practice either at the end of a shamatha session or even when you get in bed at night. Take a few minutes to rest with the natural cycle of the breath. Then contemplate the following questions, allowing whatever answers that arise to wash over you like a wave:

Is there someone in my life I feel grateful for today?
Was there something I did today that I feel grateful for?
Was there someone I had a hard time with today? Is there something about them that I can be grateful for?
Is there something about myself that I can be grateful for?

Adding in this step of contemplating someone we have a hard time with is taking our compassion practice to the next level. We are moving from focusing just on ourselves and our anxiety to contemplating the ways that even the most difficult of people can teach us new things about ourselves. We are reframing our anxiety from it being a problem to a chance to grow spiritually. It may feel a bit uncomfortable at first to add this step into gratitude practice. It's like going to the gym, working out, and pushing a bit beyond our normal comfort level; we experience some pain but ultimately, our muscles grow. By contemplating the great kindness of even the difficult people in our life, we similarly are allowing the heart to grow that much stronger.

CHAPTER 24

Joining the Unexpected with Meditation

Whatever you meet unexpectedly, join it with meditation.

—Atisha Dipamkara Shrijnana

Let's face it: we humans seek comfort. In fact, according to classic Buddhist texts, our whole human existence is defined by the desire to only seek pleasurable things and desperately avoid painful things. Often this means we're looking to external factors to determine our happiness, be it a job opportunity, a new romantic prospect, or starting a family. If only we got that thing, then, finally, we believe we'd be happy.

Fun fact: there's always going to be something new out there. We spend a lot of mental energy thinking, "When I get this new status" or "This new relationship" or "This new level of wealth" then all will be okay. One of two results then occur: we don't get the new status/relationship/wealth and as a result we feel very bad about ourselves, or we do—and now we want something else.

There is a short line in a Buddhist chant that haunts me, because it points out how many of us are "always looking for another now." Most of us haven't trained the mind to merely be present with what is going on, whether it's a subjectively good experience or a bad one, so we mentally check out and daydream about another moment in time, another "now" which we could be a part of.

Yet, at some point, life demands our attention. As Atisha points out, something shifts in our daily experience and we are thrown into a place of uncertainty. Maybe the new job falls apart, or you say something to the person you're dating and they suddenly become very distant, or your rent shoots up and you can no longer afford your home. When the rug has been pulled out from under us, instead of spinning our "What if " stories about things which may or may not happen in the future, we are being invited by Atisha to root down into our meditation practice and become grounded in the midst of the groundless situation.

Instead of fighting uncertainty and the various ways change and impermanence might hook us, we can join it with our spiritual path. This concept reminds me of lines from a poem by the Tibetan Buddhist teacher Chögyam Trungpa Rinpoche: "In the garden of gentle sanity/May you be bombarded by coconuts of wakefulness."[52]

Breaking out those two lines a bit, you're going about your day-to-day life and things are gentle and sane and then *boom*: a coconut hits you on the top of the head. Not an acorn, with a light tap that would simply be annoying but a coconut which, if it fell on your head, would knock you to your knees.

These "coconut moments" are the times when the unexpected arises in your life. For example, your lover rejects you, or a family member passes away, or you lose your job. Your heart breaks and you feel defeated. These are the times when you are completely lost and are not sure what to do next. Yet, within this time of sudden change, you are given a beautiful opportunity.

What would you do if such a thing happened to you? You have two options: (1)You can curl up in pain. You can hope that change and uncertainty leaves and picks on somebody else. This is not particularly effective in my experience. (2)You use this moment as an opportunity for wakefulness. You face your fear, anxiety and pain head-on. You look directly at it long enough to realize you have the ability to move through it.

You have likely suffered from lots of uncertainty in the past and you're still here so you know you can be resilient and strong enough to see your way through it.

While I'm focusing on uncertainty, the same advice can be proffered for any strong emotional upheaval. If you try to hide from it, you will be unsuccessful. The more you struggle against the pain, the longer you end up wallowing in it. Instead, you can dive into your turmoil and experience it fully, allowing it to wash over you like a wave, and see if you come out the other side revitalized.

When we join our meditation and spiritual practice with the unexpected, we are able to ride the waves of our life. Because there will always be unexpected and anxiety-producing situations coming up in our life, we are saying, "Can I train in remaining present and be there for them?" This is much smarter than trying to hide from them.

Can we use every circumstance of our life as a way to wake up? At some point in our meditation practice we realize that, sure, it's very helpful when it comes to changing our relationship to stress and that's great—but it's only the first step in the spiritual journey.

Building on the previous section covering bodhichitta, we need to take the long view and say we have a lifetime of training in uncertainty ahead of us, so we better open our hearts large enough to accommodate the groundlessness that arises.

In the Tibetan language, there is a word for "warrior" which is *pawo*. A more direct translation would be "one who is brave." Bravery, in this case, is not referring to someone who will go out and propagate aggression. "Warrior" is not the typical warrior who battles others. Instead, this term refers to someone who is brave enough to battle their own neurosis and strong habitual patterns. Pawo is someone who bravely addresses their anxiety and, in the midst of the uncertain times, relates fully with their present experience, coming out the other end a kinder, more compassionate person. Let's be warriors with an open heart.

CHAPTER 25

Learning to Trust Yourself

Of the two witnesses, hold the principal one.

—Atisha Dipamkara Shrijnana

Recently a meditation student of mine who we'll call Kristen told her father about how she asked for a promotion at work. "Why did you do that?" her father replied, "You're bringing too much attention on yourself. Now you're going to get fired!" Kristin was crestfallen. She was hoping for at best support, at worst mild enthusiasm but her father had hit on her worst fear, initially sending her into a spiral of uncertainty and anxiety.

Thankfully, Kristin has been meditating for a while now and noticed she could catch herself in harmful storylines and bring herself back. When she was able to reside in the present moment, she told me, she realized that the story floating in her head wasn't even hers; it was her dad's. "He had a lot of negative experiences in the workplace, always feeling like he was mistreated, and he was just projecting his experience onto me!" she said. Kristin was able to be present and aware enough to realize she didn't need to take on the anxious stories of her family.

As far as meditation success stories go, I think this one is a huge win. It's also related to the slogan, "Of the two witnesses, hold the principal one." Here, we're saying there are other people's views of what is going on with you—and then there is your own. Which do you think is a more reliable witness to the truth of a situation? The person who has a lot of fixed ideas about you, or you, who is in your own company 24/7/365? Would you rather rely on someone's idea of what happened or the truth of your own experience? Trusting the "principal witness" here refers to trusting your own understanding and insight.

This is an important slogan because so many of us are swayed by doubt. We do a presentation at work and think, "It seemed to go okay" but then we turn to a colleague and ask what they think. They shrug while staring at their phone and our heart sinks. We let their opinion of the matter subsume our initial gut reaction. This is us trusting someone else's views over our own instinct.

In Kristin's case, her father had never gone to her workplace or seen how proficient she is at her job. When she was confronted by her father's fixed view, she had the opportunity to make a choice: she could trust her own feeling around the promotion or she could be swayed by someone else's ideas. Thankfully, she chose the former.

I remember when my first book, *The Buddha Walks into a Bar*, came out. I was young at the time—in my twenties—and like most people in their twenties, still figuring out my shit (I am now too, but less so). I was proud of the book, but I was deeply insecure. So it's likely not surprising to hear that when people lashed out at me or my book, I was really hurt.

I remember one callous reviewer putting down the whole project, saying I didn't know what I was talking about and citing how I used a Sanskrit term that was actually Tibetan. (These are the nerdy critiques one gets as a Buddhist writer, by the way.) I sent it to my editor, clearly upset, and he noted that I was actually right and the reviewer was wrong. At no point before this moment had I thought to trust my own knowledge and experience. I realized I needed to look at how quickly I was swayed by the opinion of a stranger.

Over the years, I've learned to work with projections from readers. Some people might look at that book title alone and write me an email saying, "How dare you talk about meditation and drinking!" while others might write me and say "You're the best teacher alive." Both are those people's projections. When it comes to my understanding of Buddhism, I have grown over the years to trust how I am the principal witness. I know my strengths and my flaws. I know where I fall down on the job when it comes to mindfulness and compassion and I know where I am strong in integrity.

This is a subtle but beautiful benefit of going deep with meditation—we learn to trust ourselves more completely. The practice of this slogan is to be true to who we really are. You are the only person who knows yourself completely. You spend more time with yourself than anyone else ever could. So why would you trust someone else's opinion of you over your own?

Now, of course, if someone comes to you and has feedback for you, it's worth listening to it. For example, a friend takes you aside after a dinner party and says, "Hey, I don't know if you know this but sometimes your gossip is a lot to handle." Such a comment might blindside you but it might be worth looking at their statement, sitting with it, and seeing if there is truth to it.

Thich Nhat Hanh has offered a phrase we can recall when we receive either praise or blame: "You are partly right." If someone says a talk I gave was horrible, I can admit they are partly right. Sometimes I stumble and say the wrong thing! And if they say it was magic and incredibly true to their experience, I struggle with the feedback but can say they are partly right; when I'm at my best I can teach what I was originally taught and people may be helped in the ways I have been in the past.

This slogan does not say "You're perfect. No feedback necessary." In fact, the Zen master Suzuki Roshi once looked out at his group of meditation students and simply said, "Each of you is perfect the way you are. . .and you can use a little improvement." In other words, you are basically good and can trust in your goodness. You are innately whole and complete and perfect—but you might need to look at some of the obscurations blocking you from that state, such as that nagging anxiety lingering in the back of your mind.

You know your flaws and when you stop practicing mindfulness and compassion. You know when anxiety hijacks your experience and obscures you from who you truly are. Other people can offer their subjective ideas about you, but you're the only one who knows what's going on for sure. When feedback comes our way, we bring it into alignment with our inherent wisdom and see if there is truth to it. We are the witness to the situation we should trust.

CHAPTER 26

Maybe Don't Vomit Your Anxiety onto Others

"Don't talk about injured limbs."

—Atisha Dipamkara Shrijnana

I'd like to begin this chapter by apologizing to every friend who has ever had to hear me talk about a breakup. I remember one particular afternoon in my twenties when an on-again, off-again girlfriend broke up with me for the millionth time and I called my friend Brett. Brett kicked off work a bit early and met me at a bar, where I was already busy drowning my sorrows.

The story I told him about my despair, worrying about whether we would reconcile, was no different than the ones I told him about every other breakup, and ran completely in line with all the ones he was used to hearing when it came to this particular woman. Yet, he simply held space for me, offering a comforting shoulder to cry on. Only years later when I brought it up with him, he joked, "Yeah, that was really annoying of you, wasn't it?"

When we're hurt, it's a very human reaction to vomit our pain onto the other people around us. Maybe we lean hard on friends when we encounter stress in our romantic relationships. Maybe instead we play out the "What if" game with our spouse, who sits patiently on the couch while we spiral into endless scenarios about our financial issues. Maybe we complain endlessly to our sibling about our parents and the ways they stress us out. In any of these cases, we are letting our anxiety and confusion spill over from the mind and seep into our speech in the off chance that talking more about the issue may somehow solve it.

This is not how anxiety works. Our brain, the problem-solving device that it is, wants to fix whatever is stressing us out, even if it's an unfixable situation. No matter how many stories we tell—internally to ourselves or vomited aloud onto our loved ones—we will not be able to know if we will get back together with that person, when things might change financially, or when the behavior of our family members will shift. Our kicking up the same one to three stories on a loop does not affect the future. Often when we use our speech to perpetuate our anxiety, it makes the stories we tell ourselves multiply and we end up feeling worse.

One particular mind-training slogan from Atisha related to our speech is "Don't talk about injured limbs." I imagine the phrasing of this slogan arose in response the medical system in the eleventh century. I can't believe it was particularly sophisticated, so when you encountered someone who had gotten into an accident, you might notice they had lost part of one of their limbs. Even Atisha knew that you probably should not bring it up as a topic of conversation. "Hey, buddy. How'd you lose the hand?" was awkward at best.

More generally though, this slogan is encouraging us not to dwell on and speak about what we perceive to be the shortcomings of others. These shortcomings could be physical but more often are mental or emotional. For example, if your anxiety-ridden friend is freaking out about the state of the world, you shouldn't make fun of them, saying they aren't very grounded or tell them how they are acting crazy. It's not helpful to them and, as Atisha continues to implore us to do, we should aim to be helpful at every turn. We should remember others are doing the best they can and work with them from this perspective, as opposed to zeroing in on their defects.

Often when we focus heavily on the failings of others, it's a sign we aren't comfortable in our own skin. Instead of looking at our own anxiety or concerns, we turn our attention to tearing other people down, puffing up our ego in the hopes that we can feel superior to someone else.

If you have ever spotted an Internet troll, you know exactly what I'm talking about. It's that sort of energy where no matter what happens, the negative speech will flow. Someone could donate the entirety of their bank account to charity and a troll will find some way to try and verbally tear them a new one. This is not because their victim is a horrible person, but because they can't deal with what is occurring in their own mind and life.

Alternatively, when our anxiety spills out from the mind and into our speech, it might manifest as gossip. Instead of relating to our own issues, we decide to tell potentially not-true stories about others as a means of distraction: "Did you hear about Nancy? She caught her husband in bed with another woman and now she's getting divorced." This act is a classic injured limb scenario you ought to avoid. Who benefits from you telling people Nancy's business? No one! What Atisha is asking of us here is whether we can commit to looking at our speech and using it to benefit ourselves and others instead of complaining or tearing other people down.

We all have "injured limbs." It could be that you were bullied and now have low self-esteem. It could be you were raised in a household with poor money management skills and thus inherited a tendency to be bad at saving. It could be you are unskillful at love and act from a place of confusion, pursuing the wrong type of partner quite frequently. Whatever shortcomings you have, own and work with them—but don't perpetuate them. Wailing to your friends about whether you will ever love again doesn't make you feel better and drains the heck out of them. Just ask Brett.

No Complaining Challenge

While the slogan "Don't talk about injured limbs" often puts the focus on us not talking about the defects of others, many of us have a tendency to dwell on our own woes and use our speech to keep those stories about them alive. This is commonly known as complaining. We don't know how to relate to our anxiety so on some level we hope that complaining to whoever will listen will help make it go away.

My challenge to you is to take a vow to not complain for three days. Complaining drains your own life force energy and it is nowhere near the skillful behavior that can address the situation you're talking about. Complaining, quite simply put, doesn't solve anything. It only makes you feel poorly and perpetuates the stories in your head that are plaguing you.

If you are struggling with a difficult boss, for example, instead of constantly telling your roommates, friends, dates, dog, neighbors, and family about it, just notice that tendency and return to the present moment. If you want to get very disciplined about it, you can even commit to making a donation to a charity you like (or, if you're masochistic, one you abhor) every time you complain. If you have to give five dollars to the NRA every time you talk about what a jerk your boss is, you might give up the ghost on complaining more quickly.

When you make a mistake and end up complaining, don't beat yourself up. Usually, we are completely unaware of how often we use our speech in this way, so consider this a learning experience. If you only slip a few times, consider it a great victory. You are learning to drop the negative speech patterns which keep you locked in stress and are moving toward a more long-term liberated life.

CHAPTER 27

Addressing Your Issues Head-On

Work with the greatest defilements first.

—Atisha Dipamkara Shrijnana

In an excellent *Saturday Night Live* skit, Adam Sandler plays the head of a tour company, Romano Tours. While pitching his vacations in Italy, he talks about the incredible opportunities for fun and relaxation and then says, "But remember, you're still going to be you on vacation. If you are sad where you are, and then you get on a plane to Italy, the you in Italy will be the same sad you from before." I love this because he is inadvertently pointing out how no matter what we do in terms of trying to run from ourselves, at some point we need to realize our mind is our mind, no matter where we are. Anxious at home? You'll be anxious in Italy. It's the same you.

The stories we carry about what is stressing us out can change day by day, but the act of worrying and getting lost in anxiety remains with us. There will always be new things for us to be worried about—the difficult boss, or the love life gone awry, or yet another triggering news report. In order to attend to our minds and develop greater clarity and sanity, we need to look underneath the story of the day and work directly with anxiety itself.

When Atisha says, "Work with the greatest defilements first," he is referring to our largest obstacle in waking up to reality as it is. Perhaps for some people this is impatience or aggression, but if you picked up this book, I'm guessing it's your anxiety.

There are many schools of Buddhism, but I was raised in a tradition that places a heavy emphasis on the Vajrayana teachings. *Vajra* can be translated from Sanskrit as "indestructible" while *yana* is "path" or "vehicle." The indestructible element referred to here is our own wakefulness. Underneath our stress and fear lies our inherent goodness and peace, waiting to be discovered. The way we develop a deep relationship to our wakefulness is through leaning into whatever arises in our day as part of the spiritual journey.

The Vajrayana path is one marked by leaning into our obstacles. In other words, whatever stressful situation has arisen in your life, you can think, "Oh, good! Something new that will help me work with this old defilement of mine—anxiety." When we take this attitude, at first, it may feel forced, but over time, a playfulness arises and we chuckle at ourselves. We realize how today's anxiety-producing story is not so different from yesterday's or the day before. They are all manifestations of us not looking anxiety in the eye and getting to know it.

When you work directly with your stress and anxiety, treating it primarily as the purpose of your spiritual journey, you are learning to not avoid who you are. You feel what you feel, without judging yourself for anxiety arising. You sit with it, like you might an old friend who gossips and talks about nothing. You don't encourage the old friend but watch it calmly and wait for it to settle down. Once anxiety has exhausted itself, it tends to excuse itself and go away. But first you need to learn to sit with it, experience it, and not encourage it to continue on with the stories of the day.

If you are still reading this book, that says to me you are serious about working with this greatest obstacle/defilement—it has become a priority. If you haven't started meditating, please start meditating. This is *the* tool that will help us sit across the table from our anxiety and see it for what it is and not get overwhelmed by it. If you have been meditating, please consider putting this book down and being with your mind for ten minutes right now by focusing on the breath. Commit to looking at your anxiety and getting to know it so well that it no longer has control over you. Generations of meditation practitioners have done it before and they are waiting for you to join them.

CHAPTER 28

Stop Fixating on What Does Not Serve You

Abandon poisonous food.

—Atisha Dipamkara Shrijnana

Throughout our journey together, we should continue to reflect on a choice that is always available to us: we can focus our mental energy on whatever is stressing us out on a given day or we can focus it on finding contentment in the present moment. I know you've made this choice before: you're interested in the contentment piece. What Atisha is asking of us here is to do the hard work of giving up the anxious thoughts for real in order to rest in such a state.

"Obviously, Lodro," you may be thinking, "I want to give up the anxiety. But it's not so easy." On a little-known show called *The Grinder*, Rob Lowe plays an actor who played a lawyer for eight years on television—which means he believes he can now practice law in real life. This leads to him doing a number of manic things which work well on television but don't really have a place in an actual courtroom.

My favorite episode of this is when Lowe's character starts using one particular catchphrase: "But what if it wasn't?" Someone might say, "It's impossible to get them to testify" and he would pop up out of nowhere and cryptically say, "But what if it wasn't?"

Say you are newly off work and needing a drink after a harrowing week. You get home and your spouse asks you how your day was but you just wave them off, going into the other room to change. The entire commute back, you had been lost in your anxiety about whether you will land this client and whether doing so will propel you forward in your career or, as you fear, not closing the deal will mean you are at risk of losing your job. At no point did you pay attention to the commute, your spouse, or even getting undressed and now you're standing naked in your bedroom and think, "Well, my night has been taken over by this work issue."

But what if it wasn't?

Even asking yourself the question may move you away from a stuck point of view. What I am asking you to do here is to loosen up your notion that anxiety is some impossible monster out there that can enter your mind and have its way with you whenever it wants. For example, you may be clinging to your anxiety, thinking, "I need to keep on my guard or I will go soft. This is just the way it is." But what if it wasn't? Can you at least imagine a world where anxiety gets only 10% of your mental energy instead of 90%? What would that world look like?

The slogan related to this notion is "Abandon poisonous foods." I imagine that in the eleventh century, there were probably a fair amount of actual poisonous foods Atisha could caution us against. But here, what he's referring to—the real poison—is our fixation, which blocks us off from being with reality as it is.

When we spend all our mental energy fixated on whatever is currently causing us pain, we are slowly poisoning the mind and heart. If you fixate on the anxiety of the day, your jealousy toward a colleague, or your anger toward a certain politician, you are blocking yourself from the present moment by poisoning yourself with negative emotions.

On a deeper level, this slogan can refer to the notion of egolessness we talked about earlier. The ways we fixate on "me" and "my issues" without leaning into our present moment experience keep us reifying the cycles of pain we have perpetuated for decades. Meditation as a practice is not about "self-help" in the classic sense—from an absolute perspective, it is actually about undoing the sense of self, including the fixations which separate us from being who we are and being open to those around us.

The Buddhist teachings invite us to not just try and boost ourselves up and try to be great but to undo the stories we tell ourselves about why we need to be great or why we need to achieve certain things in order to be happy. We're being invited to give it all up. We can give up our fixation: our grasping and craving for things that are either impermanent or simply not going to happen; this negative habitual pattern only causes us more suffering.

The practice, in a nutshell, is to notice when you're telling yourself a lot of stories and return to the present moment. "When I'm hooked by anxiety? Impossible," you may say. But what if it wasn't?

The next time you are locked in a story about work, standing naked in your bedroom with no clue how you got there, pause. Take a breath. Then take a moment to notice three things in your environment. There's the nice lamp you got so many years ago which you still appreciate. You hear the dog snoring in the corner and it warms your heart. The sunlight is hitting your skin and feels pleasant. Already, you have shifted your mental energy from fixation to gratitude, simply by seeing what you can appreciate about the present moment.

Having taken a step back from anxiety, you have an opportunity. You can pivot into spending your mental energy not on fixation but on something new. Go in the other room and ask your spouse how her day was. Call up a friend just to check in. Move from focusing just on yourself to considering others. This gap of just one moment is long enough for us to realize we have choices for how we want to proceed. Anxiety is destined to take over the rest of your life—but what if it wasn't? What if you rested in that gap and connected to your own open heart instead? Moment by moment, gap by gap, we are training for a more meaningful and less anxious life.

CHAPTER 29

Third Eye Blind and Painful Points

Don't bring things to a painful point.

—Atisha Dipamkara Shrijnana

When I was a teenager, I was a big fan of the band Third Eye Blind. Hell, I still am. While it was not the most uplifting of their songs, "Jumper" had perhaps the most memorable refrain: "I wish you would step back from that ledge my friend." Whenever I meet with a meditation student who is about to go down the rabbit hole of anxiety and lose an hour or a day to playing the same three stories on repeat, I notice this verse rattling around my head. If only they would step back from that ledge!

The moment before we jump is when Atisha can talk us down. We don't want to cause ourselves pain, right? Well, he points out, then how about we don't bring things to a painful point? In other words, if we can't rest with reality as it is, at least don't let ourselves spin out of control over something that does not seem useful or helpful to us. This particular slogan is related to the quality of exertion: we need to exert ourselves from not falling into the same habitual patterns that cause us pain over and over again.

We Buddhists have a term for when we exert ourselves to drop what doesn't serve us: renunciation. The notion of renunciation is frequently portrayed as giving up your worldly possessions. If your clothes, books, and laptop are holding you back from being awake to reality as it is then sure, get rid of them. But for most of us, what blocks us from being wakeful and sane is our obsessive thinking, our jealousy, our anger, and so on. We ought to renounce any negative tendencies that hold us back from being open and compassionate.

The more we pull ourselves away from the ledge while we're sitting on the meditation seat, the more we will find we can do so in our everyday life. When we are causing ourselves less pain, we're less likely to inflict pent-up pain on those around us and our life will go more smoothly.

This, by the way, is the other way the slogan is often considered: we shouldn't bring things to a painful point in our relationships. There are many times when we find ourselves dealing with a difficult person in our life—even if it's our spouse—and we find ourselves baiting them like a prize fighter, looking for an opening so we can really stick it to them.

For example, while in the company of your coworker, you bring up the embarrassing thing they did two years ago, which they hoped everyone had already moved on from. While at a family function, you bring up the horrific thing your family member did twenty years ago, that everyone pretends to have forgotten. While out with your spouse, you let slip a failure that occurred in a seemingly joking way, knowing just how hurtful the experience was. Alternatively, with your partner it could be any statement that includes "Of course you do. You're just like your mother."[53]

This slogan "Don't bring things to a painful point" asks us to refrain from perpetuating our and others' suffering so that we may step away from the painful point and step into a place of understanding and compassion. When we consider this advice, we are saying that doing so is the antithesis of compassionate behavior. We shouldn't aim to humiliate or denigrate people; they are worse for it and whatever temporary feeling of superiority we may have washes away and we are only left with guilt and shame. By renouncing the tendency for one more jab, one more snide remark, or one more comment on a Facebook post, we are moving ourselves away from pain and anxiety and into liberation.

You can notice any tendency you may have to kick the hornet's nest—either in your own mind or in your relationships—and then the practice is stupidly simple: don't do it. Just don't!

Easier said than done, I know. But here's the thing: you are the Karate Kid. In the movie, our kid, Daniel, practices a series of menial tasks over and over again, which are later revealed by his mentor to actually be karate moves. Similarly, in meditation, you have been sitting there and noticing when you drift off and then coming back, instilling a short gap in between your stressful stories and acting on them.

Now you can practice the same gap you have been developing on the meditation seat and allow your reactions in the rest of your life to arise and dissolve without doing a single thing. Instead, as odd as it may seem in the moment, you can pause and just be present with your experience. Having rested in that gap, you can even see if you can offer the person in front of you some small kindness, offering a compliment or thanking them for something they have done in the past. It's mutually disarming and shifts the dynamic drastically. Stepping back away from anxiety, you (just like the Karate Kid) become swift and skillful in working with the opponent in front of you, moving the situation from one of tension and pain into one encompassed by compassion.

CHAPTER 30

Advice for Beginning and Ending Your Day

Two activities: one at the beginning, one at the end.

—Atisha Dipamkara Shrijnana

No one wakes up wanting to give their day over to anxiety. Yet, all too many of us do so. If some of Atisha's other advice around the concept of emptiness has felt amorphous, here, he is giving us something very practical to help: begin and end each day with a moment of heart-opening practice.

Let's pretend for a moment that you wake up in the morning and immediately reach for your phone, open your texts or email, and find someone is already asking for your attention. This sends you into a cycle of anxiety and your mental to-do list begins to spiral. You haven't even placed your feet on the ground, yet you're floating into a stressful abyss of "What if . . . " thinking.

Let's Groundhog Day this one and do it again. You wake up in the morning and before you even touch your phone, you take a breath and check in on your body. Scanning from the base of your feet on up to the top of your skull, you notice where there is some tension and gently relax those muscles. You contemplate gratitude for the goodness in your life. You take a moment to contemplate the people you care for and wake up your heart, touching your bodhichitta. You can set an intention: "I will bring my mindfulness and compassion into the rest of my day." Then you look at your phone.

With one to two minutes of practice time, you have already set your day in a different direction than you might have otherwise. You are relaxing into reality as it is, being in the body, and resting in the present moment. You are connecting to your own open heart. These acts give you fortitude and resilience so that when the stressful triggers come your way (and they will!) you are able to not be shaken by them. This moment of starting your day with bodhichitta is the first part of what Atisha is referring to when he advises, "Two activities: one at the beginning, one at the end."

The activity at the end of the day is one of reflection. While brushing your teeth or getting ready for bed, you can take a moment and ask yourself, "How much was I able to live from the perspective of mindfulness and compassion?" If you had a day where you were genuinely connected to bodhichitta and were kind and compassionate to those around you, awesome! Rejoice in that. Let yourself feel the goodness of having really exerted yourself in a positive direction. If you put your toothbrush down and think, "I gave up two minutes after checking my email," well, tomorrow's another day. You can try again.

The nice thing about this slogan is that it's a daily practice we can employ over time so that gradually, moment by moment, we are aligning our mental energy away from constantly giving into anxiety and stress and more toward presence and open-heartedness. As we transition into our final section, we move from the Mahayana path of compassion and emptiness into more of the Vajrayana path, considering our life from a point of sacred view. We will look at how to work with anxiety in a myriad of situations in our life but before we do, I want to emphasize that these slogans can and should be revisited regularly. We can write one on a sticky note and put it somewhere we will regularly see, or write a different one on each day of the calendar so we remember to contemplate them. These slogans Atisha offered hundreds of years ago may be pithy, but if we apply ourselves to them, they reveal themselves to be full of practical, down-to-earth advice on how to live a more meaningful and wakeful life.

PART FOUR

Rubber Meet Road: The Practical Application for Your Anxious Lifestyle

CHAPTER 31

Taking Mindfulness on the Road

Mindfulness isn't difficult; we just need to remember to do it.

—Sharon Salzberg, *Real Happiness:*
The Power of Meditation[54]

The notion of mindfulness can get a bad rep because it's an inward-focused activity. If you are mindful of your breath, or your eating, or even showering, it's just about you, right? The answer is yes, but only if you've managed to completely isolate yourself. This is because the moment you get up from that activity and go to the gym, or browse a clothing store, or open up social media, you're tasked with the challenge of applying mindfulness to your interactions with others. The question becomes: instead of spinning into anxiety, can we slow down and treat our day with the respect it deserves?

In this section, we will look at the nitty-gritty details of our day—especially the ones which might trigger stress and anxiety—and see if we can apply our mindfulness and compassion to these scenarios to live a more peaceful life. The fundamental shift from our previous work together is that instead of looking at anxiety as a problem, we consider it a part of our spiritual path. The Vajrayana perspective is that we can transmute the experience from viewing anxiety as an obstacle to one of sacred opportunity. We will look at how we can step back from our habitual momentum and ways of doing things and instead rest in our own buddha-nature or innate wakefulness. Through our meditation practice, we are learning how to take a step back and rest in space so we can best understand how to step forward in the rest of our life from a place of appreciating how magical life truly is.

Through the foundational practice of meditation, we have begun to tune into our life like a radio signal. We realize the vibrancy and beauty of being present. The more we train in being present, the more we become discerning about the people we spend our time with, the way we engage our work, how we approach travel, and even our financial transactions. We learn that we are enough, we have enough, and we are inherently awake—and that under whatever layers of anxiety may exist on a given day, our own basic goodness is there, ready to shine like the sun on a moment's notice.

Sometimes, in order to bring these principles into our life, it becomes a matter simply of getting out of our own way. *Prajna* is a Sanskrit term which can be translated as "wisdom," but more directly as "superior knowing." It's the type of knowing that takes place when we are able to loosen up our ego and be present with the way things are, as opposed to how we thought they would be or how we suspect they should be.

When I'm leading a guided contemplation practice for my online community, I often start by inviting everyone into a few minutes of settling the mind by paying attention to the breath. This practice allows us to relax into the present moment. The more we are able to relax into the way things are, the more clearly we can hear the little voice inside us. Prajna is the wisdom which is present when we get out of our own way and move beyond our thinking mind.

When prajna is infused into our mindfulness and compassion, it becomes something extraordinary and transcendent. When we aim to be generous, we're removing the "me-ness" from the equation and simply tuning into what's going on and how to be of benefit to others. Wisdom dawns when we are able to simply be with things as they are. When we make space for our wisdom, we learn how to show up in the world in a way that is meaningful and beneficial to ourselves and to others.

One traditional Buddhist analogy is that wisdom and compassion are like two wings of a bird; we need both in order to soar. When we connect with our wisdom mind, we are not just becoming more skillful in our activity but also more compassionate. Remember when I shared about my meditative walks around my neighborhood? Sometimes, I find that the easiest way to let go of my own self-involved storylines and get out of my own way is by looking around and considering the strangers passing me by. As a formal practice, you can simply let your gaze rest on someone and make the aspiration, "May you be happy." See what it feels like to make such an aspiration for someone you may never speak to. Speculation around what happiness looks like for them might arise but then turn to someone new and repeat the aspiration. We don't need to get lost in our stories about them; the practice is to remain open and present to as many people as possible, to appreciate the sacred opportunity to open to the world around us.

Here, we are switching from our self-involved framework to include the many people around us. If you want to be miserable, you should focus a lot of your attention only on your own struggles. If you want to be happy, consider the strangers around you. There's an old saying that a stranger is just a friend you haven't met yet. While it sounds trite, it can be true. We may never meet this person or exchange long-winded stories about our upbringing, but we can cultivate a heart of friendship for everyone around us. If nothing else, when we apply our wisdom mind to the simple moments of our life, we drop out of our stressful storyline and are more available to the rest of our day.

CHAPTER 32

The More Money We Come Across, the More Anxiety We See

> *On the whole, we should regard money as mother's milk . . .*
> *very precious. At the same time, mother's milk can be given*
> *away, and we can produce more mother's milk. So we*
> *shouldn't hang on too tightly.*

—Chögyam Trungpa Rinpoche, *Work, Sex, Money*[55]

I've never met someone who did not experience stress and anxiety as some part of their relationship with money. We all have patterns we unintentionally inherited from our parents or caregivers. We have our own ways of spending money which develop over time. Some of us even carry secret shame around how generous or not generous we are, or that we financially support institutions that are not the best for the environment or to their workers. If you can find someone who has a 100-percent-clear understanding of how each dollar they spend affects the economy and is in touch on an intuitive level with how they feel about each financial transaction,

I'd love to meet them.

Yet, we can't ignore our relationship to money just because it might bring about anxiety. Instead, we can approach our understanding of money and wealth from the perspective of inquisitiveness and generosity. Remember way back in Chapter 2 how we fleshed out the three realms of anxious thought (personal, interpersonal, and societal)? In a similar fashion, let's look at our inner relationship with money, how we can wield it to benefit the relationships in our life, and then explore how our financial decisions actually affect society.

Personal

For a long period of time, when I would go to the ATM to withdraw money, I would feel a wave of anxiety. At the end of a transaction, when they flashed my account balance, I would throw my hand up so as not to see it. This is about as willfully ignorant as one can be, literally hiding from our financial reality, hoping it will go away as we swat at a button that will make it disappear.

Of course, I realized my relationship with this everyday situation was neurotic as hell and sought to address it. For me, that means regularly reviewing my bank transactions online in the comfort of my own home (as opposed to receiving this news with a line of strangers behind me) and tracking my income and expenses on my phone so I keep to a budget. Just because this works for me—with my unique balance of poverty mentality and inherited champagne taste that's been honed over decades—does not mean it will work for you and your own money relationship.

The larger point here is that each of us has to have a relationship to money which is based in reality. From a foundational vehicle point of view, this means relating to our relationship with money so that it does not cause us or other people around us harm. Some of us blow through vast sums of cash, not understanding how we spend it. Others are well-trained in pinching pennies and are afraid to spend money for fear we will never make more of it. As Chögyam Trungpa Rinpoche points out in the quote opening this chapter, we can realize that money is incredibly precious, but it is much more fluid and ever-changing than we might normally conceive of it. It makes no sense to go to extremes in our relationship to it, and when we find that we are going to one end of the spectrum or the other, we should look at those patterns as a way to loosen the hold they have on us.

As noted in previous chapters, meditation is an incredible tool for cultivating discernment. As you've found, when you are meditating, you can notice the same storyline play out a hundred times in a row. For example, you sit down to meditate on a Sunday morning and in your head, you replay the scene of pulling the ridiculous bar receipt out of your pocket. Instead of coming back to meditating on the breath, you immediately leap into self-aggression and anxiety mode, chastising yourself: "You jerk! Why did you buy all those people drinks? You don't even know them! And now how are you going to pay rent?" At some point, you notice that you've drifted off and return to being with the breath. The same storyline might come up, or it might look a little different: "You took a cab both ways last night?! Where do you think the money for that is going to come from?"

After beating yourself up and then coming back to the present moment over and over again, at some point you may realize, "Oh, I don't like when I spend money like that. It gives me anxiety. Maybe I shouldn't do it." Once we've discerned we want to cut out a certain activity, we apply the discipline of following through and doing that thing.

In addition to cultivating good patterns, we also need to realize how money will not bring us everlasting happiness. It's not like we make a certain amount and say, "Oh, good. Now I'm set and never need to think about money again." For many of us, money weighs pretty heavily on the mind over the years and our relationship to "enough" shifts and changes. So another aspect of looking at our personal relationship to money is to see what our expectations are around it.

If we base our life around this notion of "I'll be happy when . . . " and end the sentence with "I have X amount in the bank" or "I can buy a house," we are bound to be live a life marked by anxiety. Happiness is not something that can be acquired by financial gain, much less what money can buy us. We need to look at our personal relationship to money to see through this fallacy and wield it for the benefit of others.

Interpersonal

In the Mahayana tradition, generosity is said to be the virtue that produces peace because it liberates us from only thinking about ourselves and opens us up to the possibility of considering the well-being of others. There are any number of ways to express generosity, ranging from offering our time to a neighbor who could use some help moving furniture to offering our resources, such as lending someone our car so they can visit their parents.

Often, when we think of generosity, we think of offering money. Having discerned (even just a little bit) what we would like to cultivate and cut out of our life, we likely have a sense of how we like to spend our money. We feel bad when we buy expensive shoes we never wear. We feel good when we give a homeless man a few dollars. Thus, we can form a commitment to do less of the former, more of the latter, and focus on generosity when it comes to our relationship to money.

In addition to giving to charitable organizations we believe benefit society, we are put in everyday situations where we're asked to look at how generous we want to be. Anytime we pay the bill at a restaurant, are confronted with a tip jar at the local coffee shop, or settle up at a bar, we experience a moment when we are invited to contemplate how generous we want to be.

Generosity is not an equation where you give something and are "correct" and feel good about yourself. It's a situation where we go a little bit beyond our comfort level, acknowledge that someone may be in need, and offer from the openness of our heart. Generosity is not limited to money, but I'll give you fair warning that if you try to tip your waiter with a warm hug, they may look at you funny.

Societal

Finally, there is the basic truth that however we spend our money, we are impacting the world around us. If I walk into a bar and order an Auchentoshan, neat, I'm not just paying for a glass of (damn good) scotch. I am supporting a local business—my local bar, Makers, as opposed to the half dozen bars nearby—so the owners of this establishment can put a certain amount of money aside to pay rent. I am tipping a bartender who likely holds multiple jobs to get by. I am supporting everyone who contributed to the making of this fantastic drink, ranging from those who brewed it at the distillery in Clydebank, Scotland all the way down to the people who delivered it to the bar a few days earlier.

And it's not just me and my beverage of choice, but each of us with every purchase we make, be it a shirt which is either made in a decent way or on the backs of child labor, a hamburger we order which affects cows and their farmers as well as our ecosystem, or even your decision to purchase this book, which affects my ability to produce such work in the future. Every purchase we make is a moment of connection to a wider world around us and can (and likely will) effect the state of our mind.

Like many Buddhist teachings, the notion of interdependence isn't some fancy dogmatic idea; it's simply the truth. We are all connected. Our actions affect other beings, which has a ripple effect throughout society. While I realize this may sound intimidating, we need to move beyond intimidation to best consider how we use our money to support the world in a way we feel good about.

For example, the next time you are handed a bill, you can take a moment to notice the flavor of your mind. Are you wincing before you open it? Do you feel good about what you ordered? Take a breath. Look at the bill. Continue to tune in to any emotions coming up in your body. Some may be rooted in decades-old patterns. Others may seem surprising and new. You don't have to sit in meditation for twenty minutes to do this; simply take a moment or two to notice what comes up for you.

If you are offered the opportunity to tip, notice what amount comes to mind. You may be feeling a bit tight around money or you may be feeling magnanimous. Take a moment to turn your attention to the person you are tipping. See if you can put yourself in their shoes and imagine their lifestyle for a moment. See if you experience any sense of open-heartedness toward this person. Then tip in a way which helps you cultivate generosity. Notice the flavor of your mind after doing so. I imagine the predominant sensation won't be anxiety. When we learn to bring even the smallest of financial transactions onto our spiritual path, we are looking to them not as something dirty but as nothing other than ways to wake up our mind and heart. This is the Vajrayana view: whatever we meet in our life can be an opportunity for wakefulness.

CHAPTER 33

A Stress-Free Work Environment

Rick: *I congratulate you.*
Victor: *What for?*
Rick: *Your work.*
Victor: *I try.*
Rick: *We all try. You succeed.*

—*Casablanca*

One area of our life which undoubtedly gives us stress is the workplace. Despite the title of this chapter, I can't promise you the secret to having a stress-free work environment, but there are ways to minimize our anxiety about work, to establish boundaries, and even to feel successful. Can we consider the workplace to be a part of our spiritual path, perhaps even an area wherein we can wake up to our innate wisdom? In a word, yes.

In American society, sometimes "success" is a term which denotes that someone is financially well-off and has somehow worked the system to the point they don't have to work much at all, or only do work they completely enjoy. Yet, if you asked many of the people you admire if they considered themselves successful, you may be surprised by their response. Many Hollywood stars, well-paid "thought leaders," and politicians are plagued by the same self-doubt, anxiety, and worry that you are. They may have more money or more flexible work hours than us, but they may not consider themselves "successful" in the way we envision.

So, what is success? In my personal opinion, success in one's work life is based in the Mahayana view where we do our best to help people. If you come to work with the view that you can benefit others and aim to do so to the best of your ability, whether you check out people's groceries for a living or work in real estate, you are still doing good work. Instead of defining success as something we need to get from external factors—be it money, power, or things we can gain through either—we could think about it as having a sense of healthiness and delight from knowing we are aiding the world around us.

In this way, success comes down to letting go of our anxious storylines long enough to show up for others—whether it's our coworkers, employees, or clients—with a modicum of respect and appreciation for our shared humanity. Even the most difficult of clients has the same basic goodness you and I have; recognizing it and attempting to discover it alongside them is a gift that we can offer. Whoever is right in front of us becomes the most important person in the room and the best way to serve them is to hold enough space for their own wisdom and wakefulness to arise.

When we consider the office as a laboratory for our compassion and wisdom to shine, our work becomes the training ground for our spiritual path. Chögyam Trungpa Rinpoche once said,

"Work is also something *real*, just as much as spiritual practice. So work doesn't have to have any extra meaning behind it, but it is spirituality itself."[56] We don't have to get some perfect job where we can consider ourselves spiritually sufficient or finally able to help others; we can look to our current circumstance and, by being present, see if there are ways we can help others right now. There is nothing "extra" we need on top of such a practice.

There is something very earthy and humbling about looking at a situation and just doing what needs to be done. When I was running the meditation studios I cofounded, MNDFL, I would see the front desk staff doing an excellent job hosting new students, showing people around, and rearranging the cushions in the meditation space. But then I would notice the dishwasher was dinging and the clean mugs needed to be unpacked. The best thing for me in that moment was not to deliver the best meditation talk or chat up a student about their experience—it was to unpack the dishwasher. And unpacking the dishwasher is glorious in and of itself. The moment I think I am too good to put away the mugs is likely the moment I should step down as a Buddhist teacher.

There is an old Zen saying: "Before enlightenment, chop wood and carry water. After enlightenment, chop wood and carry water," meaning that even after the highest levels of meditative awareness are attained, you still have to relate to your daily life. To illustrate this point, there is a story where the Zen master Shunryu Suzuki Roshi was approached by a meditation student who went into great detail explaining an experience he had of dissolving into spaciousness. He then asked Suzuki Roshi for feedback or advice. "Yes, you could call that enlightenment," Suzuki said, "but it's best to forget about it. And how's your work coming?"[57]

I do understand how some (many) of us have inconsiderate people and difficult situations at work who stress us out. When work is overwhelming, we don't have to just take it. Even the seventeenth-century Spanish Jesuit philosopher Baltasar Gracián noted, "Know how to say 'no.' One ought not to give way in everything nor to everybody. To know how to refuse is therefore as important as to know how to consent."[58] In other words, the Buddha never gave a "Lay Down and Be a Doormat" sermon. We can be compassionate and still establish boundaries that protect us so that we do not burn out.

People will email me after a talk I give on this topic and try to explain how their work situation is unique and they simply can't say "no" to the various demands that emerge. After a long back-and-forth, I discover they haven't been having any conversations about the matter with their boss or their coworkers, only with me. This is a big problem which ignores the reality of our work environment. Let's say you are one of ten people in an office. That means you are 10 percent of your work society. Ten percent of any society has a strong voice. Even if we are 1 percent or 0.1 percent of a society, we have a voice. By engaging in constructive conversation, we may be able to shift our work environment.

The next argument I am often hit with is that in this person's workplace, there is no room for such mindful conversations. In fact, they might ask me, "How can I avoid lots of negative talk and gossip?" My favorite parable in this regard is about a rabbi whose neighbor overheard him telling a story about a relative who was arrested for stealing. This neighbor thought the rabbi was talking about his own son and began to spread this gossip to everyone who would listen, which as you can imagine was quite a few people.

When it was revealed that the story of theft was not, in fact, about the rabbi's son, the neighbor came forward and apologized, asking if there was anything he could do to make things right. The rabbi took him up to the top of a hill on a particularly windy day and handed him a pillow. "You can slit the pillow," he responded. The neighbor did so and feathers flew out into the air. "Now you can go gather up the feathers and put them back in the cover and give them to my son," he said. The neighbor realized that it was impossible. Similarly, there was no way to take back gossip. I often think of this parable when I am tempted to gossip, as I know how in most environments, it is just as tricky to undo rumors as it is to stuff those feathers back into the pillow.

When you are confronted with gossip, you could respond in a straightforward manner with something along the lines of "Sorry to interrupt, but I just don't like to listen to gossip," or "I'd rather not hear stories about coworkers which might make me think negatively about them." The tricky part is that you may need to move away from the conversation should this person continue. As discussed in the chapter on the trap of doubt, when we don't feel very good about ourselves and are lost in anxiety, we end up gossiping and slandering others. Knowing how we may have perpetuated these bad behaviors in the past may allow us a sense of understanding and compassion for those who continue to fall into this pattern.

These conversations we have at work often need to be brave. In order to counter a materialistic, stressed-out or gossipy game plan in the office, we need to work with our mind and heart so we can be above such negativity. In all of the situations above we are learning to move away from stressful triggers long enough to reconnect to our own sense of basic goodness. When we realize our inherent goodness, we bring our own energy of kindness, decency, and respect to every interaction we have from the moment we walk through the door to the last email we send at night. If we can do so we will experience success, maybe not in a conventional way but in a deeply spiritual one. We thus make our workplace a training ground in transmuting stress into wakefulness.

CHAPTER 34

Taking Your Foot Out of Your Mouth

Swiftest horse cannot overtake the word once spoken.

—Chinese proverb

The Vajrayana view is that whatever we encounter can be treated as sacred. What starts in the mind often will manifest in our speech and activity. If the mind is open and present, then our speech and activity will flow seamlessly from that state. If the mind has been taken over by anxiety, then our speech and activity will move in that direction. That means that every time we open our mouth, we can think of it as an occasion to promote our own wakefulness or to drop the ball and cause ourselves and others harm.

Traditionally, there are a few no-no's as articulated by the Buddha when it comes to expressing ourselves in conversation. Going all the way back to the foundational teachings he offered, he taught what is known as the Eightfold Path which helps us wake up from our suffering. One aspect of the Eightfold Path is known as Wise Speech. Wise Speech means we acknowledge that words can create happiness or suffering and we can try to use our speech in a helpful manner. This means we should avoid:

lies

gossip

slander

harsh words

abusive language

speech that divides people from one another

idle speech (words we may offer simply to fill space)

Now I'm guessing you may look at this list and think, "Okay, I don't really do much of that." But when we truly analyze our behavior, we might see we have work to do. For example, when you got in late the other night and, when confronted by your parent, roommate, partner, or kid about when you arrived, you might have made it sound like you got in earlier than was truthful. Or a friend asked you about someone you used to date and you said a few things you knew would put a particularly negative image of them in your friend's head. These are but two of a million ways we could, unintentionally, break from Wise Speech. That is why it has been a brilliant 2,600-year-old discipline for us to practice.

Of course, it's not that the Buddhists have cornered the market on how to have a good conversation. Every etiquette book under the sun has advice for us on this topic. Although it may now be considered incredibly outdated, *Vogue's Book of Etiquette* in 1948 issued an excellent list of things to avoid, which includes:[59]

speaking in languages other people
present can't understand

leaving members of the group out of conversation

self-indulgent monologues

picking topics only certain members
of a group can speak on

categorical pronouncements on
moral or ethical questions

attacking another person's religious tradition,
nationality, political party, or race

Again, much of this is common sense until we get swept up in conversation at a party and wake up the next day very anxious, having said that alienating thing to a complete stranger.

Having mentioned a number of things we could avoid in conversation, I'd like to share a few suggestions for things we could actively do in conversation to move from anxiety into a realm of feeling uplifted. The first thing we could do in a conversation is to deeply listen to the other person. As the Chinese proverb goes, "Two good talkers . . . not worth one good listener." Just listening to someone and asking the right questions allows them to relax into conversation in a meaningful way because they know they will be heard.

Deep listening is a genuine practice. In the same way we focus on the breath in shamatha practice, here the object of our attention is the sound of the other person's voice. This means when thoughts arise, such as "I agree!" or "I have to share this story with them," not only do we not interrupt but we also acknowledge those thoughts and return to listening to the other person. We don't plan what we will say when it's our turn or strategize how to fix the problem they are presenting to us—we just listen. When it is our turn to speak, we will have a fuller understanding of what is going on and will be able to speak from the present moment and our own intuitive awareness, which will end up being much more skillful.

The next thing might be to offer aspects of your life you find meaningful. We don't need to brag about our many accomplishments. Instead, reflect on something you found fulfilling that day or week. Thus, it's likely not "I got a promotion" coming out of your mouth (although there's nothing wrong with sharing this news with an old friend) but "I discovered this little dog park yesterday and I was so touched by watching the dogs and their owners play." This sliver of vulnerability, through revealing the little things we find meaningful, often shifts a conversation to a very positive place.

I learned this last part about conversation not from a traditional Buddhist text but from my friend Dev Aujla. Dev is the sort of person who constantly has five different projects going at a given time because his interests are so varied. At this time, he has an interesting role as a recruiter for a large firm, he just released his second book on how to get a meaningful job, and the love story about him and his wife is so beautiful, it was just featured in the *New York Times*.

Yet, if you ran into him at a party, he would never lead with his many accomplishments. He would tell you about a class he is taking through a group he found online, or an interesting book reading he just attended, or about how his mother was recently in town and what they did together. These are the things Dev gets excited about, and thus these are the things that he contributes to form a heart connection with other people. When offered the chance to relate with someone through conversation, he leads with a sense of vulnerability. As a result, Dev has a lot of friends who consider him genuine and they feel like they can be open and honest with him.

Now, sometimes a conversation takes a nasty turn and the other person asks us something we are uncomfortable addressing. We don't need to go along with their train of speech just to be a good sport. If someone asks, "Why did you leave your job so abruptly? It was a dream job!" you might want to take the advice of the *New York Times* columnist Philip Galanes by responding with the question, "Why do you ask?" He said, "It's my go-to for nosy questions. It says, nicely: 'Why do you think you have the right to ask me this?' Many people will come to their senses and redirect the conversation."[60] Alternatively, while coteaching a long meditation retreat with my friend Susan Piver, I came up with an acronym for this situation in her honor, SUSAN:

Stop. Pause the conversation to make it clear the dynamic in the conversation has changed.

Understand: Ask questions of this person to get to the heart of why they are going in this conversational direction. If not "Why do you ask?" then perhaps, "What made you think of that?" or "Is this the best time to discuss the situation?"

Speak clearly and precisely in response.

Acknowledge what they said: "Am I getting what you said to me correctly?"

Notice how you feel: After some back-and-forth to clarify where this person is coming from, do you feel uplifted or dragged down? If the latter, it might be a good idea to move on to another conversation.

Which brings us to ending a conversation. Even a simple "I'd love to catch up another time" acknowledges the other person in a meaningful way. If you don't ever want to see them again, even an "It was so interesting getting to know you" is at least truthful. Maybe it's just me, but I think being able to explore the eccentricities of anyone is, at the very least, interesting.

A Side Note on Email

Many of us have stared at a computer screen, reading and re-reading a message before clicking send, to make sure our perspective can be heard properly and clearly. This can stress us out.

Why? Well, this message is being received by someone and we have no sense as to when they will see it, how they will react when they see (yet another) email in their inbox, or how they will respond when they click it open. Even though we have come to rely on this form of communication for everything from a "Hello! How are you?" note to the sharing of big news to swift business transactions, many of us haven't considered how to wield this tool of communication in a skillful manner.

In short, we can treat email as an extension of speech. It is a wise idea to always consider the words you offer will be received by someone sans tone of voice or facial expressions, so we have to choose our words carefully.

One thing I've found important in my work is to remember that behind every email is a suffering human being. They are going through their own things today, large or small. If you receive an email from them which is curt, they might just be having a hard time and it has nothing to do with you. As for sending, before you click Send, just take a moment to consider how your note and (to the best of your ability) the tone of your words may be received and see if you need to edit anything out. It may also be helpful to say only what you would say to someone—or even about someone—if they were standing right in front of you.

Another point to consider relates back to the emotions work we have done earlier in this book. I don't recommend sending anything in a fit of anger or any other strong emotions. We can sit with those emotions instead, taking them to the meditation seat. Confucius once declared (long before email existed), "If you are happy, do not promise anything. If you are angry, do not mail a letter." In other words, don't let your emotions dictate you saying something you wish you had not said. Because you can't predict where your words will go, you need to choose them wisely or end up creating more stressful situations for yourself down the road.

Whether we are sitting down to dinner with our spouse, about to click Send on an email, or are meeting new people at a party, we can begin to view our speech as sacred activity. Stemming from the foundational teachings of the Buddha on Wise Speech, we can learn how not to perpetuate suffering (both our own and that of the person we're talking to) and even begin to engage our speech in a way that is beneficial and kind. When we rest in our own experience of basic goodness, we are more likely to see people for who they truly are, to compliment them, and to offer words of encouragement. When we dwell in anxiety, we may end up grinding our teeth, waiting for the other person to shut up so we can finally talk only about ourselves and our issues. Having worked with the mind, we find we have the freedom to wield our speech as a tool to benefit ourselves and others, deepening heart connections and allowing this very moment, this conversation, to be the experience that transforms us from anxious to awake.

CHAPTER 35

Mistakes and Apologies

Since we're human beings, we make mistakes. We cause others to suffer. We hurt our loved ones, and we feel regret. But without making mistakes, there is no way to learn.

—Thich Nhat Hanh, *How to Love* [61]

We all make mistakes (Lord knows I have). What do we do when that happens? Wallow in anxiety and guilt, letting them eat away at us? Or step up and lean into the nervousness we may have around the situation and attempt to mend fences, perhaps even apologizing?

Whenever I have unintentionally hurt someone or put my foot in my mouth, I think of our friend from the eleventh century, the Buddhist master Atisha. Not because he was known to do so (although he was human so he must have) but because of one final slogan I want to offer: "Drive all blames into one." Meaning, we need to look at our role in any given situation and own our shit. It's not easy to drive the blame for whatever goes wrong in our relationships solely onto our shoulders, but it's often a good starting point if we want to move through the mistakes which were made and, ideally, make amends.

As I mentioned before, I'm writing much of this book during the coronavirus pandemic in 2020. During this time, millions (millions!) of people are quarantined in their homes and many of us are not used to being in such tight quarters with loved ones for so many weeks at a time. My wife and I actually get along very well and are used to working from home together, navigating the space, and cleaning up after one another. Yet, after the first month, I was cleaning out the cats' litter box and she began to play the world's worst couple game: "Why Are You Doing It That Way?" Apparently, washing the litter box out in the kitchen sink is not as preferable as doing it in the toilet and when she brought this up, I snapped at her, letting her know in specific terms that I had not asked for her help.

She retreated and I was immediately filled with regret, having overreacted to her nudge. Having realized that my snapping at her came from a place of speediness and experiencing a lack of trust, I apologized. Not surprisingly, she was quick to forgive. By apologizing for even this minor transgression, I was exposing myself in a slightly vulnerable way, which all too often leads to a shared willingness to be vulnerable together and heal from that place, as opposed to a place of defensiveness. In this way, driving all blame onto oneself is actually a practical way to shift the dynamic away from aggression toward others.

Apologizing—whether it's about the cat litter or something much more serious—is a practice in humility and in loosening our fixed points of view. It's a true spiritual practice, in my opinion, which includes a renunciation of ego and willingness to connect from a place of authentic regret. It's something I have become better at over the years, ranging from apologizing to my parents for being a brat when I was younger to apologizing to women who I was callous or hurtful toward in my twenties. Representative John Lewis, during an interview, once said, "We need to evolve to that plane, to that level where we're not ashamed to say to someone, 'I love you. I'm sorry. Pardon me. Will you please forgive me? Excuse me.'"[62]

Another way to look at this idea is through the lens of a maxim from Baltasar Gracián: "Do not turn one blunder into two."[63] The first blunder in a situation can be small, like forgetting a friend's birthday which came and went without a remark, or vast, like sleeping with that friend's spouse on said birthday. In either case, you have made one mistake. It is best not to continue to make mistakes on top of it. Here, the second blunder would be not directly and appropriately dealing with situation and not making amends.

I am fond of pointing out that whatever understanding I have of Buddhism comes from studying at the feet of great wisdom teachers and, if there is a mistake to be made on the spiritual path, I have made it. Sometimes they have been in my business dealings, partnering with people I likely should not have, or in my romantic life (particularly back when I was single). Whenever I was able to make amends though, I have sought to do so, even if doing so doesn't always look like I thought it would.

Mistakes happen. They are a part of life. Ideally, the more familiar we become with our mind and our basic goodness through meditation practice, the less we are spaced out and make errors in the rest of our life. I do make fewer and less harmful mistakes than I used to as a result of my meditation practice even, say, seven or ten years ago. But when a blunder is committed, we can heed Atisha's advice and own up to it, drive the blame squarely onto our own shoulders, and follow up with Baltasar's advice by relating to the situation appropriately.

But what to do when you are the one who is harmed by another? Unfortunately, on a relative level, Atisha's advice only goes so far. You can examine your role in whatever altercation that has occurred, but if you find no blame to drive onto yourself, you might need to either hold your seat or speak out from a place of kindness. As for holding your seat, the etiquette columnist John Bridges once wrote, "When a gentleman has been subjected to a conscious insult, either in public or in private, his response is simple: because he is a gentleman, he says nothing at all."[64]

Holding your tongue is hard to bear sometimes, but if someone is not at a point in their own life where they can see the offense caused, or you point it out and they aren't conscious enough to attempt to make amends, you may choose to wish them well and not spend any more time with them than you have to. This can at times feel better than the alternative, which is to demand an apology. Why? Well, as the New York Times columnist Philip Galanes once pointed out, "Receiving apologies we are forced to demand is about as satisfying as baking our own birthday cake."[65]

Alternatively, there are times when you suspect that not speaking out about a situation will only cause harm to linger or even be perpetuated by this person in the future. In that case, you can look at the situation and ask, "How can I address this harm from a place of kindness?" Kindness isn't about just being nice; often, it looks like us saying something another person doesn't want to hear but having everyone's best interests in mind. Sometimes, when we feel harmed, we want to lash out and make the other person feel bad about themselves. They may learn from the situation or they may not, but at least we temporarily feel vindicated. That is not really kindness because we're not trying to benefit all parties concerned.

Instead, by asking this question, you are framing your response around finding a way that this person may learn from the pain they have caused and, through kindly pointing it out, allow them to reconsider acting in such a way in the future. Even saying, "I'm not sure if you know this, but what you did hurt me," opens up a dialogue, particularly compared to the shorter, more vindictive version: "Fuck you, asshole." By either holding your tongue or speaking out, you are not writing anyone off or closing your heart to them; you are considering their humanity and seeing how to make things right from a place of bodhichitta.

This aspect of holding your seat or speaking out, all while keeping an open heart, is at the root of the question of basic goodness. If someone has wronged you, whether it is forgetting your birthday or sleeping with your spouse, this does not negate that they are basically good. They possess the same seed of wakefulness, kindness, and open-heartedness you do. Yet, the fact that they are not in tune with their goodness and are very much lost in their own confusion and suffering leads them to act in ways which are harmful to themselves and others. We have all been there.

Here's the tricky part: just because someone is not acting from a place of goodness does not mean we give up on them. In fact, as Chögyam Trungpa Rinpoche once said, "The essence of warriorship, or the essence of human bravery, is refusing to give up on anyone or anything."[66] Not giving up on someone is a very advanced view. Just because someone is in pain, and thus acting out and causing other people pain, does not mean they are lost to the world and unworthy of our compassion.

If you can remember the basic goodness of others in this moment, you are more likely to empathize with them and generate a heart full of compassion. And at the same time, this doesn't mean you are meant to fix them or spend your time making them your new meditation project. You can hold someone in your heart, wish them well, and also know you may not be the best person for them to interact with. This may free you from your anxiety about the relationship to a large degree.

Then, if this person comes to you looking to make amends, you are in a better position to consider their pain and apology than if you had merely written them off. Like a hot coal, your own anger and bitterness does not hurt anyone around you when you clutch it tight; it hurts only you. Better to let it go and move on with your life, apology accepted.

CHAPTER 36

Rough Travels

Some, wearied by their travels far from home,
Must suffer separation from their wives
And children whom they love and long to see.
They do not meet with them for years on end.

—Shantideva, *The Way of the Bodhisattva* [67]

For some of us, travel can bring up a lot of anxiety. Whether we travel for work or play, the tension starts to mount well before we board the airplane. In the days leading up to it, our suitcase comes out and we begin to anticipate the things we will forget to pack, we run government-level scientific equations in our head about how long we need to travel to the airport, and we are lost in fear about what will happen if we botch some leg of our trip.

All too often, when travel anxiety arises, we need to take those three deep breaths and remember to be very patient with ourselves. One particular piece of advice which has stuck with me comes from Sharon Salzberg's book *Real Happiness at Work* where she offers three magic words to keep in mind when we find ourselves lost in stories about what might go wrong: "Something will happen." I will make my flight or I won't make my flight and will make other arrangements. Something will happen. It will be okay.

When I ask you to be patient with yourself, you may roll your eyes at me (and that's okay). Translated from the Sanskrit word *kshanti*, "patience" in this context is not something based in just waiting until you get to do what you want to do. It means to fully relate with a situation, even if you find it incredibly frustrating or uncertain.

The great Tibetan Buddhist teacher Dudjom Rinpoche broke patience out into three ways we can practice it: remain unflappable when wronged, happily take on the pains of life, and aspire to a true understanding of reality.

Whether you are used to having to practice patience while traveling by plane, train, or automobile, you can bring this principle to mind to ensure your travel experiences are opportunities for you to grow on your spiritual path.

Air Travel

Perhaps you are the sort of person who feels that unless your flight goes exactly as planned, it must be someone's fault and this person really ought to be dragged through the streets by horses for wronging you. This moment when you are the last person at baggage claim and you realize your bag simply isn't coming, it's been lost, and you have no idea if you will ever see it again, can be really painful. And yet, it's the perfect moment to open to Vajrayana view: a brand-new practice opportunity has been delivered to you. Instead of shrinking from this situation, you can soften into your new reality and respond with patience, which will get you through this situation with much less stress. When Dudjom Rinpoche said we can practice patience by remaining imperturbable when wronged, this may not be exactly what he was referring to, but it's a modern and frequent example of a unique practice opportunity.

Whether you are boarding a plane, stuck in the middle row with Mr. Loud Snorer on the right and Ms. Armrest Stealer on the left, or are being snubbed by the airline attendant, there are lots of opportunities to catch yourself when you're about to spiral and remember this is the opportunity for practice. John Bridges once pointed out that while on a flight, we become "a member of a small community, a community that has its own rules and its own codes of behavior" for the duration of the trip.[68] As the old saying goes, "The way a person does one thing is the way they do everything." If you show up in these smaller instances of travel from a place of anxiety and impatience, then you are reifying that pattern so you will show up for the most important aspects of your life from that perspective. Catching yourself in the moment and moving toward patience allows you to plant those seeds so you show up patiently for even the most difficult aspects of your life. Furthermore, patience is a quality often lacking in this sort of society, but if you can bring it to the forefront of your imagination, it often has a ripple effect in such close quarters.

Trains

A moment ago, I mentioned three ways Dudjom Rinpoche talked about patience including how we could happily take on the pains of life and perhaps you thought I was going too far. Let's take an all-too-common example of when this form of patience is helpful.

The moment when you are riding the subway to an important meeting and it comes grinding to a halt due to an unexplained delay is frustrating at best, terrifying at worst. In this moment, can you pause and flip the script from "obstacle to what I want to have happen" to "practice opportunity" by looking at those other individuals in the subway car, trapped in the same situation you are, with a moment of connection and empathy? Doing so may lead you to a bit more patience and understanding and get you through the situation that much better.

Whether you're on a cross-country train ride or just trying to get to work on the subway, we can slow down and act in a compassionate manner. Having an awareness how we are all in it together can be heartening and moves the focus from "me" and "my concerns" to "we're doing what we can, collectively." *Something will happen.* Those three magic words are a good thing to remember at such times.

Automobiles

The final form of patience Dudjom Rinpoche recommends is when we look at life on its own terms, often translated as something very much in keeping with Vajrayana view: "aspiring to a true understanding of reality." This means that when your travel plans go south, you can drop everything and look to reality not as you wish things were going, or how they used to be, but as they are, in an unfiltered way. If you can be with your situation as is, you have a chance to see your situation more clearly and respond from a place of true wakefulness.

For a low-key example, if you are waiting in the car trying to be a good, patient spouse and your partner is taking a very long time to get ready for your trip, you might be tempted to increase your driving speed along the highway in order to make up for lost time. Yet, this is putting both of you in unnecessary danger and you are now testing the patience of your spouse (something I try to do as rarely as possible) as well as that of the nice elderly woman you cut off who is now flipping you the bird.

Instead, when we embark on a car ride, accept it will take whatever amount of time Google says it will take, perhaps give or take a few minutes, and relax. Beating the clock isn't a good look on anyone shy of an NBA player. Better to accept reality as it is and lean into it patiently.

A less low-key example would be that your travel plans fall through entirely and you are left in a groundless and uncomfortable situation, stranded somewhere unforeseen. In this moment, can you look to your new reality and relax with things as they are? If you have been practicing meditation regularly, the odds are in your favor.

With all of these travel rules, the common denominator is twofold: By using travel as a means to practice patience, we feel better about the experience, while the second aspect is we start to become more understanding and compassionate to others.

An On-The-Spot Practice for Traveling

The next time you are impatient while commuting, take a moment to come into your body. Do a quick body scan, notice the weight of your body on the earth and the gentle lift of the spine, and relax the muscles in your face by letting your jaw hang open. Notice how you are breathing, allowing it some time to relax into its natural cycle. Then raise your gaze and simply relax your mind for a moment. Rest with no object of your attention.

Now look at the people around you. Take a moment to contemplate how they may be feeling and whether you have any of those emotions in common. If you see someone having a hard time, silently make the aspiration, "May you be peaceful." See if you can relax into empathy and understanding for them, alongside the realization that we're in this together.

CHAPTER 37

True Love in Relationships

In the end, there is no desire so deep as the simple desire for companionship.

—Graham Greene, *May We Borrow Your Husband?*[69]

The one thing Graham Greene failed to mention in the quote above is that out of the desire for companionship comes a lot of anxiety. Let's look at how to relate to the stress modern dating and relationships can bring up and see our way through it to connect to true love which flows seamlessly.

Dating

Aziz Ansari's book, *Modern Romance*, details a phenomenon that occurs when people feel bogged down by the problem of too many choices when it comes to potential romantic mates. He has a beautiful chapter in which he describes a visit to a home for the elderly and bears witness to story after story of people who met their spouse because they lived on the same block, went to the same small school, or even lived down the hall from them. Back then, people's worlds were relatively small and the choices available for a potential spouse were limited.

There are endless ways we can search for find love nowadays. Comparatively speaking, Juan, a community member at MNDFL, was using the meditation app Insight Timer and noticed there was a woman who was meditating at the same time he was regularly—but in Norway. You can imagine my surprise when he introduced me to her a few months later, having connected with her through the app and invited her to come stay with him to try out a relationship. If we are at the point where we're meeting potential mates on meditation timer apps, you know we've entered the realm of limitless possibilities.

With limitless possibilities seemingly comes limitless stress. How do you know someone is a good match? By a photo of them holding a puppy (or God forbid, a tiger) on a dating app? Their flirtatious banter over texts? Actually talking to them and hearing the sound of their voice? I may be old-fashioned but these days, the only way to get out of our head about what someone *might* be like is to see what they actually are like by sitting down with them in person.

When it comes to bringing our meditative mind into the somewhat stressful dating equation, we need to realize that whoever we're sitting down with deserves our presence from the moment we begin a courtship (whether it be meeting on an app or at a party) all the way through to the dissolution of our time together.

On a practical level, this means when you sit down with this person you can tune into your body and notice how you are showing up for them. Even how you hold your posture can invite or dismiss the presence of the person right in front of you. You can try taking a dignified but relaxed posture just like you would in meditation.

One way to think of this is to reflect on advice I received when I was a kid. My meditation instructors would tell me to meditate in the way a king or a queen might sit upon their throne. Even thinking of this advice in the comfort of my home makes me sit up a bit better at my laptop. Balancing relaxation with openness in our physical form shows the person we are receptive to who they are and what they are saying.

To go a step further, you can practice deep listening, focusing your attention on the conversation and being fully present to it, as discussed earlier in this section. Instead of focusing on your fixed ideas of "Where is this going?" or "Do they like me?" you can drop your agenda and get genuinely curious about your date. Whether you suspect you will want to date this person for years or merely one evening, see if you can be present to the point where you let go of those thoughts about the future and find something you can enjoy about their company. Even if you're not itching to marry the person at the end of the night it does not mean you should space out; you can find great enjoyment in just getting to know another person.

Now a moment ago, I mentioned setting aside our fixed opinions about someone and if I were you, I'd try and fight me on this topic. "But Lodro," you may say, "it's actually really important to me that a potential spouse . . . " and you can fill in the blank with any number of descriptors.

Let's do a quick exercise: make a list of everything you would want in an ideal date. Write it out on paper. You can list their physical attributes, their disposition, and even their hobbies. Then take a long look at it, soaking in what you wrote. Finally, crumple up the piece of paper up and safely burn it.

While it might seem a bit dramatic, many of us get lost in our fixed expectations of what we think we need in a person in order to be happy dating them. This fixation means we are not actually spending time in an open-hearted way, being inquisitive about the people we're meeting, because we're constantly looking to check a number of boxes to determine whether this person is the "ideal" match we've been searching for. By burning this list of expectations, we are letting go of our habitual ideas of what we want and are more available to the world and the people around us. We are more willing to try to connect to the basic goodness of everyone we meet. Try it and see if you are more open to meeting new people and if you are willing to simply explore what form of connections arise.

Long-Term Relationships

I'll open this section by saying it's not just you. It's literally every person in a long-term relationship on the face of the earth. At some point, you wake up next to the same person, whether it's the one-thousandth or ten-thousandth time, and your first thought is not "Wow, who is this magical creature?" but "Why can't they ever turn off their own alarm?" Yes, you've moved to the point where you might have started taking your once-glorious date turned long-term romantic partner for granted.

It's normal. You're not a monster for getting annoyed at your spouse over the small things in your shared life. My dear friend, author, and Buddhist teacher Susan Piver tells a great story of coming into the kitchen and getting annoyed the moment she saw her husband of many years standing there, stirring the soup wrong. Did you know there is a right and a wrong way to stir soup? Apparently, there is and Susan's husband hadn't learned the difference. Does this mean she doesn't love him? Of course not. It's just a golden example of how our long-term romantic partners are often the best grist for the mill of our spiritual practice, as they will likely be the trigger point for a whole lot of neurosis. Rainer Maria Rilke noted that it's one thing to fall in love and another to maintain it when he said, "For one person to love another: that is perhaps the most difficult of all our tasks."

Your spouse serves as a fun-house mirror for you, not only reflecting back but also distorting some of the confusion and afflictions already coming up in your own mind. How many times have you snapped at your partner and then admitted (to yourself or to them) that it's not them, you just have a lot of stressful stories going on in your head?

Why are our spouses often the recipients of our ingratitude and scorn? We supposedly love these people! The short answer is that over the months or years, we have slacked off by letting go of the basic tools we aim to develop during our meditation practice; we no longer work to be gentle, present, or inquisitive with them. When we were first courting this person, we treated them as an honored guest in our home. Now they can at times feel like the unwanted guest from out of town.

When we first start dating someone, everything is an exploration. We are actively listening to every word they say, soaking in the culture of this new person. Because everything feels fresh, we think they are the most unique and interesting person we have ever met.

As we get to know this person, we think we, well, know them. The totality of who they are. We believe them to be a fixed entity who never changes and never develops new interests. For example, when my wife and I first started dating, she turned me on to everyday love scenes depicted by the Korean artist Puuung. On her next birthday, I surprised her with one of these scenes as a phone cover. But a while back I noticed that she had discarded it for something new.

Should I have gotten annoyed at my spouse because she scorned my gift after a few years of use? Of course not. I realized she may be sick of always looking at Puuung after years of doing so. She is an evolving, changing beauty of a woman whose interests, like so many aspects of her being, have likely shifted over time. The bigger issue than a discarded gift is that I have not investigated what artists she is into *now*. As you can see, what could be a mundane annoyance on my part actually revealed to me one of the many ways I was taking my partner for granted. I realized that if her interest in artists had changed, her musical preferences, the friends she holds in high esteem, and her fashion choices likely have shifted around me all while I was holding on to the idea of her as one entity I "know."

We have talked extensively about egolessness and emptiness; we think we are one thing and the world around us is another thing. We believe both exist in a solid and fixed way. In fact, though, you know you are constantly changing. You likely would not argue with me that you are not the same person you were years ago and you will likely be a very different person years from now. Physically, mentally, and emotionally, you are constantly in flux.

This solid sense of "me" you have is really a conglomeration of five aggregates: everything you believe to be your physical form, your feelings, your sense perceptions, the way you form concepts about what you perceive, and a coordinating sense of "me" which makes everything about you, you, you. So, when you look at your boyfriend, it's your concept of your boyfriend that you see, not his true nature. Yet, he is similarly a shifting and changing conglomeration of these five aggregates and is seeing you through his concepts. In the midst of this confusion, nothing is as stagnant as we conceive it to be. We're all so much more fluid than what we normally believe. Dropping our fixed ideas of one another is a step into sacred view.

The next step into sacred view is realizing that the only fixed part of your long-term partner is their basic goodness. If you can, even when you are pissed off, remember how this person you love, at their very core, is good, smart, kind, and strong, then you might actually be more willing to cut them a break. You might be willing to become freshly inquisitive with this person, seeing them for who they are today as opposed to who you think they have become over the years.

One easy way to drop into this mindset is to really listen to your partner, seeing if they bring up topics you haven't heard before and investigating them. They might mention a new podcast they are listening to, or a new store they visited, or even a new client at work. These are doorways to explore how they are engaging their world a bit differently. From these access points, it's nice to communicate how you have heard them, clarifying and building on the conversation by adding your own reflections. Echoing back in this way lets your partner know you respect what they said, that you are making an effort to get to know them anew, and you want to understand them as they are right now. While it may seem corny, my wife and I will sometimes look over at one another while having morning coffee and bluntly ask, "Who are you today?" This simple question frees our partner from the box of fixed expectations we have set up in our heart and allows love to flow freely.

While I have been talking a lot about showing up in a mindful manner and becoming inquisitive about the other person, a lot of mindfulness and compassion within a relationship actually comes down to simply relaxing enough so you have the time and space to enjoy each other. When you are truly present with your spouse, anxiety about what the future may bring dissolves. In the same way you might return to the breath during your formal meditation practice, you can return to whatever you are doing with your partner. In these intimate relationships, our presence often communicates more than words can truly express. The silence of morning coffee together grows to feel comfortable, because we are relaxing together and giving one another space to simply be the totality of who we are.

CHAPTER 38

When Our Loved One's World Falls Apart

Love can have an enduring quality when we make it a conscious spiritual practice.

—His Holiness the Karmapa, Ogyen Trinley Dorje,
The Heart is Noble [70]

There's everyday anxiety and then there's life-has-completely-fallen-apart anxiety. Those words might mean different things to different people: it might be a job loss or the sudden death of a loved one or an unexpected breakup or divorce. In any such situation, when the rug has been pulled out from under us, one emotion which might emerge alongside stress and anxiety is grief.

Recently, I received an email from someone who sat a meditation retreat with me a number of years ago. It was quite long and included a lot of heartbreak in it—her own but also feelings of despair and fear for society. As the email culminated in a fever pitch, she wrote me, "All the people with big hearts? They commit suicide" and I have to say, reading those words brought tears to my eyes.

I like this woman a lot. She's tough and fair and called me an asshole once when a particular teaching I offered was too glib for her taste. But I responded, according to her, with humility, and the experience brought us closer together so much so that when she wrote me about having such a hard time, I felt deeply empathetic.

It's really hard to live in our world today. Thich Nhat Hanh wrote, "Never in human history have we had so many means of communication—television, radio, telephone, fax, email the Internet—yet we remain islands, with little real communication between us."[71] Collectively, it feels like we desire things to only move faster and be more efficient and yet simultaneously mourn human-to-human interaction. Like teenagers rebelling against their supportive parents, we rage against the same planet we need in order to survive. And, at some point, it gets to be too much for some people and they can't cope anymore and they struggle to the point of wondering what they even have to live for.

I've had suicidal ideation in the past and work with a number of meditation students who have as well. The idea of "Is this life even worth it?" is scary and I'm glad so many of us are in therapy, which can provide tools for looking at our own minds and seeing our way through our suffering. The thing about suicidal ideation though is that it's often a private topic. People experience shame for having these types of thoughts so it can be your father, your sister, or your close friend and you might never know just how much they are struggling.

Wish as we might, we cannot wave a love wand and have those we care about be healed, but we can offer an ongoing presence of love which, as the Karmapa points out at the top of this chapter, has an enduring and spiritual quality to it. One way to care for the people in our lives is to simply show up for them with an open heart and mind.

When we spend a lot of time with someone we love and cherish, we make basic assumptions about them. Unless they are in tears over a downturn in their career, a loss of a relationship, or some larger grief, we usually assume they are fine and treat them as such. Yet everyone is suffering, so we must be kind. These people in our lives, with their big hearts—we have to look out for them during this really tough time in our society. To take our loving-kindness practice off the cushion, here we can contemplate what these people we love are actually going through.

Bring to mind someone you cherish: a friend, partner, family member, or even a pet. Imagine them sitting across the table from you. Stay with this image for a minute. How is your heart, right now? Perhaps open, tender, or filled with gratitude. This is a big part of why we bring these people to mind in loving-kindness practice—even their image helps spark the fire of love within us.

In the traditional practice, we take it a step further: we recite aspirational phrases for them. We say "May you be happy" and pause. In that moment, there's a chance your mind goes to such thoughts as "I hope they have a good birthday later this week" or "What *would* it take for her to be truly happy?" These are not bad thoughts: we are contemplating this person in our life through a new and curious lens. We are seeing them fresh and relating to their struggles. Simultaneously, we are wishing they be free from any suffering they might be encountering.

Loving-kindness practice trains the mind and heart to be open and inquisitive about the people in our life. When you next see this individual, notice if you listen more to them, or hold more space in the conversation for them to reveal parts of themselves you may not normally notice. In the Vajrayana path, we practice ways of being with what is, as opposed to having to do a great deal or manipulate our experience. Here, you are no longer aiming to do loving-kindness practice, you are embodying the ideals of the Vajrayana by simply being in a state of wakeful love.

Meditation practice is wonderful, but we must realize that we are truly practicing mindfulness and compassion principles for the rest of our life. We consider those people close to us, big hearts and all, and learn not to take them for granted. We see their suffering and their kindness, both, and embrace the totality of it. Thich Nhat Hanh once said, "To love someone, you need to be there for them one hundred percent. The mantra 'I am here for you' says that I care about you, I enjoy being in your presence. It helps the other person to feel supported and happy."[72]

All too often, when we slow down and consider the life of our loved one, we reveal there's a lot that we tend to gloss over. The skillful action here, having considered the perspective of another, is to then engage them from a place of compassionate inquiry. We can start with "I am here for you" but some questions I have found helpful to follow up with are:

> How can I help?
>
> What is the fear around this matter? Is there a way I can help address your fear?
>
> How does your situation make you feel?

The more inquisitive we become with this loved one, the more we can work with them to unearth and heal their suffering. In addition, it is helpful to celebrate who they are as a person. Sharing at least three positive qualities you have observed in them can bring about a sense of appreciation and being seen.

Loving-kindness is a way to safely consider these loved ones from the meditation seat. The more time we give to considering them, the more perspective we have to skillfully support them long-term. These people with their big hearts can really suffer at times, so it is up to us to show up for them as genuinely and with as much consideration as possible.

And if you are the one who has had their world fall apart? Perhaps this, right now, is the moment to reach out to one of those good friends with a big heart. You can even say, "I am suffering. Can you help?"

CHAPTER 39

Anxiety and the Modern Family

If you think you're so enlightened, go spend a week with your family.

—Ram Dass

There is one particularly lovely and stressful community each of us participates in from the moment we are born: our family. Unlike your religious community, your book club, or your friend group, you don't get to pick which family you participate in. You're born into it and it's yours until the moment you die. Some of us couldn't imagine not speaking with our family every week, while others are far removed from engaging them. The extent to which we want to interact with our family, and how we define it, is up to each of us, but it's something we can't really avoid participating in, one way or another.

The television show *Modern Family* depicts the antics of one large family which consists of a number of iterations: the grandfather/father (who is on his second marriage and has a stepson and a son in that second marriage), a daughter (who is part of the stereotypical "nuclear family" as she is married to a man and they have three children together), and a son (who is married to another man and has adopted a child).

The basic premise of the show (and my long-winded explanation of it) proves how these days family is what we make of it; it's not about who came out of whose vagina. It's more fluid than that. The etiquette expert Millicent Fenwick, way back in 1948, defined the word *household* as "a unit, a group of people joined together, living under the same roof."[73] I like this way of thinking of a household because some of us may consider our roommate family, or our close friends, or the dog we adopted. However you personally define your family and household society, you likely already know (by having read this far into the book) the importance of figuring out meaningful ways to show up for it and recognizing the inherent goodness of your family situation.

There are many stages of relating to our family members. As a child, we learn from them about what is appropriate and kind and what is not. They are our first spiritual teachers, for better or for worse. In my case, my parents were about a decade into their Buddhist practice by the time I was born. As a result, they were able to embody the principles of mindfulness and compassion in ways I internalized subconsciously without them having to tell me those are things one might consider a priority in life. For that, I am very thankful. For some of us, our elders were extremely kind and present; for others, they may have been unkind or absent.

As we get older and venture out into the world, we are exposed to many new perspectives which might call into question some of the values we were raised with. A dear friend of mine, Yael Shy, runs the Global Spiritual Life community at New York University. Each year, she and her team offer spiritual support for all students, but I can tell that she feels particularly tender toward incoming freshmen. There is a moment when eighteen-year-olds show up at college and quickly realize that the values they held dear growing up are not shared by everyone.

As we continue to mature, we might reflect on the principles we were raised with and incorporate them into an adult version of the spirituality we experienced as a child or move into a completely new exploration of a different tradition. In either case, we have this moment as adults when we realize the values we hold dear are partly formed by our family but have also been influenced by friends, teachers, mentors, spiritual leaders, and more.

Then we go home to visit our family. We think we have a new lease on life, a new understanding of the nature of the universe, and we think we know what makes things tick. We are ready to display the new, evolved version of ourselves to our family. What happens then? If you're like me, the moment you walk through the door, you fall into the same patterns you were raised with and, ten minutes in, you might be complaining that you don't want to take out the trash in the same tone you did when you were a surly teenager.

This is the basic rule of karma: we have strongly ingrained habitual ways of considering ourselves, our loved ones, and the world around us, and these ideas propel us to do the same sort of things over and over again, unless we cut through that particular pattern. In the long-term Buddhist view, we have been playing out the same patterns of passion, aggression, and ignorance with various versions of our families for lifetimes. That said, you don't need to believe in multiple lifetimes to know that when you're complaining like a teenager to your dad, it's because you used to complain like a teenager to your dad.

We all have our own deeply ingrained patterns with our families. It's the default setting for how we relate to each other, who holds what role, and how we express love to each other. There are specific dynamics between parents and children, siblings, cousins, and so on. And if we're not careful, we will continue to reify these patterns and dynamics out of sheer laziness.

If life was a video game, I think the boss awaiting you at the end of the final level would be your family dynamic. Many families carry a "This has worked for us thus far; no one has killed each other" mindset and don't really want to budge from business as usual.

However, if you are sick of relating to your (negative, not-so-helpful) family patterns in the same old way, you can remember the advice offered before by Chögyam Trungpa Rinpoche: "Everything is predetermined . . . until now." The next time you are on the phone with a family member or see them in person, you have a unique opportunity to change the flow of business as usual.

You can show up for your family member and embody mindfulness by deeply listening and becoming gently inquisitive about their experience in an attempt to unearth a deeper layer of conversation than what you normally get to experience together. You can hold space for them to talk about what's ultimately on their mind, without offering advice or judgment, and show your compassionate heart. If you're stuck, quite frankly, you can go somewhere new and try something different with them—eat a new food, go for a walk—anything you have never done together before. There are a million ways to shift our family dynamics into new territory, but we have to rouse ourselves out of our habitual mindset to do it.

When we show up for our family members in this way, we are entering uncertain territory and it can sometimes be scary. You have an idea of who this person is based on your many years together. By changing the dynamic of your relationship, you are wading into the landscape I like to call "Is that so?" Is this person you consider to be stubborn, or artistic, or successful, actually that way? Are they always just like that? By showing up with mindfulness and compassion for your family member, you are, in essence, dropping your preconceived idea of who you think they have been and opening up to who they truly are.

In this way, we are connecting with their basic goodness. We are seeing them for their innate wakefulness, kindness, strength, and wisdom, as opposed to boxing them in with ideas about who they should see romantically or what they should do for work. The more we connect with their basic goodness, the more abundant we both feel. The knotted-up negative patterns we have come to rely on for years slowly unravel and we are left with the opportunity to get to know each other in a completely fresh manner.

Even if we do not get to see our family often, we can reach out to them in ways we experience to be meaningful and continue to emphasize showing—as opposed to telling—about, our experience of mindfulness and basic goodness. We are learning we can transcend "doing" the practice and simply embody it, which is part of the Vajrayana path. By learning to start fresh over and over again in coming back to the breath in our meditation practice, we are in fact training to start fresh and drop our preconceived ideas of our friends, our family, and all of our loved ones, so that we can continue to plumb the depths of our shared humanity and goodness.

Conclusion

It's important to stay present because in this moment right now we have clean drinking water, clean air, there aren't any bombs blowing up around us right now, we have our health . . . So the way to bring yourself back into this moment is to simply breathe. That's the greatest tool.

—RuPaul Charles, *Masterclass*

If you take nothing else away from this book, I hope it's that you are not your anxiety; you are innately whole, complete, and good as is.

The practice advice is meant to get us thinking and trying new things to benefit ourselves, the people we encounter, and the world overall. But first, we have to recognize both how anxiety is not something we are powerless against and also that goodness is always available to us.

As RuPaul points out, the quickest way through our anxiety is to relax into the present moment and to simply breathe. The greatest tool I can offer you for your anxiety is shamatha, but in each of the practices we have gone over, we always begin by turning our attention to ourselves. Whether we're doing mindfulness of the breath practice or loving-kindness practice, it's important that we take good care of our being, offering ourselves the kindness and love we need in order to flourish. This kindness and love we offer ourselves as part of the Hinayana path is the foundation which allows us to then show up more authentically for others.

Throughout our exploration of mindfulness—both of the breath and of strong emotions—we realize the importance of becoming kinder and friendlier to ourselves. Pema Chödrön once said, "Developing unconditional friendship means taking the very scary step of getting to know yourself. It means being willing to look at yourself clearly and to stay with yourself when you want to shut down. It means keeping your heart open when you feel that what you see in yourself is just too embarrassing, too painful, too unpleasant, too hateful."[74] In other words, the act of meditation and the joy of applying it to the details of our life shows us all of who we are. We get to know the wonderful and creative parts of ourselves and the anxious and stressed-out parts as well. The more you look at your relationship to yourself, the more you see you can accept every aspect of who you are. You are innately whole and complete. You are basically good. The foundational vehicle is based in realizing you don't have to cause yourself and those around you harm and connecting more fully to your innate goodness.

When you relax into the present moment, you notice that underneath your stress is a tender, vulnerable heart which longs to love. As part of the Mahayana path, we explored the Four Immeasurables: loving-kindness, compassion, sympathetic joy, and equanimity, alongside a number of heart-opening practices, allowing you to switch the focus from solely focusing on your anxiety to considering the care of others.

These teachings on the relative side of the Mahayana path on compassion are balanced with the absolute teachings on emptiness, and I have to thank our dear friend Atisha for his slogans which help us remember that we can drop the stories we tell ourselves and relax into reality as it is. Many of the mindfulness and compassion concepts we studied are punched up to the nth degree when we study the mind-training slogans, including our gratitude, patience, and exertion when opening the heart to others.

Finally, we touched on the Vajrayana teachings by looking at our everyday life as a training ground for transforming our anxiety. When you relate to your money, your love life, your work environment, or even your morning commute from the perspective of practice, you will likely realize you have a choice: you can spend your mental energy lost in thought or come back into the present moment and find wakefulness on-the-spot.

As part of the Vajrayana view, we are learning we can practice meditation to the point where we begin to live it. We aren't trying to do mindfulness because we are, now, mindful people. These qualities become the hallmark of our existence. Then, because we understand how we get stuck and cause harm to ourselves and others, we start to see how other people get stuck too and our heart opens to them. We yearn to help the world around us. We become pillars of compassion, offering our heart and presence whenever possible wherever we are. We don't practice meditation to become better meditators. We practice to become familiar with our own innate goodness, to connect with the goodness of others, and to realize the goodness of society overall.

On an outer level, this book is a guide to living a life where anxiety doesn't rule the mind. On a more inner level, it's a guide to a more mindful and compassionate life through Buddhist principles. On a secret level, it's about realizing our own basic goodness, developing confidence in it, and seeing it in others so that we realize the goodness inherent in society.

If we can learn to love ourselves and others and see everyone's goodness, we can change the world around us. Through bringing our mindful, compassionate game face to every aspect of our personal life, to interpersonal relationships, and to each society we take part in, we create a ripple effect and move the world in the right direction. But these are just words I offer. It's up to you to take action—to do the practices in this book and see if they change you for the better.

The good news is that you have tremendous power to help others. You possess everything you need within you to take back your mind, to change your relationship to anxiety and ultimately make this world a better place. Thank you for your practice. I'm here doing it alongside you. Let's leave our negative patterns behind and change this world together.

Endnotes

1   Emma Pattee, "The Difference Between Worry, Stress and Anxiety," *New York Times*, February 26, 2020, https://www.nytimes.com/2020/02/26/smarter-living/the-difference-between-worry-stress-and-anxiety.html.

2   Katie Hurley, "Stress vs Anxiety: How to Tell the Difference," PsyCom, https://www.psycom.net/stress-vs-anxiety-difference.

3   Katie Hurley, "Stress vs Anxiety: How to Tell the Difference," PsyCom, https://www.psycom.net/stress-vs-anxiety-difference.

4   Tom Ireland, "What Does Mindfulness Meditation Do to Your Brain?", *Scientific American*, June 12, 2014, https://blogs.scientificamerican.com/guest-blog/what-does-mindfulness-meditation-do-to-your-brain/.

5   Tom Ireland, "What Does Mindfulness Meditation Do to Your Brain?" *Scientific American*, June 12, 2014, https://blogs.scientificamerican.com/guest-blog/what-does-mindfulness-meditation-do-to-your-brain/.

6   Gil Fronsdal, *The Dhammapada: A New Translation of the Buddhist Classic with Annotations* (Boston, MA: Shambhala Publications, 2005), p. 1.

7   Thich Nhat Hanh, How to Love (Berkeley, CA: Parallax Press, 2015), p. 23.

8   Chögyam Trungpa Rinpoche, *Shambhala: Sacred Path of the Warrior* (Boston, MA: Shambhala Publications, 2007), p. 52.

9   Emmanuel Vaughan-Lee, "Radical Dharma: An Interview with angel Kyodo williams," *Emergence*, https://emergencemagazine.org/story/radical-dharma/.

10   Sharon Salzberg, *Loving-Kindness: The Revolutionary Art of Happiness* (Boston, MA: Shambhala Publications, 1995), 93.

11   Zenju Earthlyn Manuel, *The Way of Tenderness: Awakening through Race, Sexuality, and Gender* (Boston, MA: Wisdom Publications, 2015), 45.

12   Chögyam Trungpa Rinpoche, *Training the Mind and Cultivating Loving-Kindness* (Boston, MA: Shambhala Publications, 1993), 43.

13   The Dalai Lama. *The Dalai Lama Book of Quotes*, ed. Travis Hellstrom (Long Island City, NY: Hatherleigh Press, 2016), 23.

14   Thanissaro Bhikkhu (trans.), "Vaca Sutta: A Statement," *Access to Insight* (BCBS Edition), July 3, 2010, http://www.accesstoinsight.org/tipitaka/an/an05/an05.198.than.html.

15   The Karmapa, Ogyen Trinley Dorje, *Interconnected* (Somerville, MA: Wisdom Publications, 2017), 41.

16   The Karmapa, Ogyen Trinley Dorje, *Interconnected* (Somerville, MA: Wisdom Publications, 2017), 235.

17   Dza Kilung Rinpoche, *The Relaxed Mind: A Seven-Step Method for Deepening Meditation Practice* (Boston, MA: Shambhala Publications, 2015), xxiii.

18   Thich Nhat Hanh, *How to Fight* (Berkeley, CA: Parallax Press, 2017), 14.

19   Phrases for Stress, Joseph Goldstein, 10% Happier App (2018).

20   Pema Chödrön, "Pema Chödrön on Waking Up—and Benefiting Others," *Lion's Roar*, February 25, 2017, https://www.lionsroar.com/no-time-to-lose/.

21   Cleo Wade, *Where to Begin* (New York: Atria Books, 2019), 148.

22   bell hooks, *All about Love: New Visions* (New York: William Morrow, 2000), 95.

23   Thich Nhat Hanh, *Essential Writings* (Maryknoll, NY: Orbis Books, 2001), 149.

24   Chögyam Trungpa Rinpoche, *Shambhala: Sacred Path of the Warrior* (Boston, MA: Shambhala Publications, 2007), 12.

25   Adreanna Limbach, *Tea and Cake with Demons: A Buddhist Guide to Feeling Worthy* (Boulder, CO: Sounds True, 2019), 183.

26   John Lewis, interview by Krista Tippett, *On Being with Krista Tippett*, March 28, 2013, https://onbeing.org/programs/john-lewis-love-in-action-jan2017/.

27   Thich Nhat Hanh, *Essential Writings* (Maryknoll, NY: Orbis Books, 2001),97

28   John Lewis, interview by Krista Tippett, *On Being with Krista Tippett*, March 28, 2013, https://onbeing.org/programs/john-lewis-love-in-action-jan2017/.

29   bell hooks, *All About Love: New Visions* (New York City: William Morrow, 2000), 4.

30   Sharon Salzberg, *Loving-Kindness: The Revolutionary Art of Happiness* (Boston, MA: Shambhala Publications, 1995), 28.

31   Acharya Buddhakkhita, "Metta: The Philosophy and Practice of Universal Love," *Access to Insight* (BCBS Edition), November 30, 2013, https://www.accesstoinsight.org/lib/authors/buddharakkhita/wheel365.html.

32   The Amaravati Sangha (trans.), "Karaniya Metta Sutta: The Buddha's Words on Loving-kindness," *Access to Insight* (BCBS Edition), November 2, 2013, https://www.accesstoinsight.org/tipitaka/kn/khp/khp.9.amar.html.

33   Sharon Salzberg, "Keeping Anxiety in Perspective," *Ten Percent Happier*, February 25, 2020, https://www.tenpercent.com/meditationweeklyblog/keeping-anxiety-in-perspective.

34   Sharon Salzberg, *Loving-Kindness: The Revolutionary Art of Happiness* (Boston, MA: Shambhala Publications, 1995), 40–41.

35   Rev. angel Kyodo williams, Lama Rod Owens, and Jasmine Syedullah, *Radical Dharma: Talking Race, Love, and Liberation* (Berkeley, CA: North Atlantic Books, 2016), 96.

36   Thich Nhat Hanh, *Essential Writings* (Maryknoll, NY: Orbis Books, 2001), 103.

37   The Dalai Lama. *The Dalai Lama Book of Quotes*, ed. Travis Hellstrom (Long Island City, NY: Hatherleigh Press, 2016), 10.

38   Thich Nhat Hanh, *How to Fight* (Berkeley, CA: Parallax Press, 2017), 103.

39   A number of this organization's resources can be found at instituteforcompassionateleadership.org.

40   Pema Chödrön, *When Things Fall Apart: Heart Advice for Difficult Times* (Boston, MA: Shambhala Publications, 2000), 107–108.

41   Susan Piver, *The Four Noble Truths of Love: Buddhist Wisdom for Modern Relationship* (Somerville, MA: Lionheart Press, 2018) p. 146.

42   His Holiness the Dalai Lama and Archbishop Desmond Tutu with Douglas Carlton Abrams, *The Book of Joy: Lasting Happiness in a Changing World* (New York: Avery 2016).

43   Thich Nhat Hanh, *How to Love* (Berkeley, CA: Parallax , 2015), 8.

44   Pema Chödrön, *Welcoming the Unwelcome: Wholehearted Living in a Brokenhearted World* (Boulder, CO: Shambhala Publications, 2019), 118.

45   Sharon Salzberg, *Loving-Kindness: The Revolutionary Art of Happiness* (Boston, MA: Shambhala Publications, 1995),150.

46   Thich Nhat Hanh, *Fidelity: How to Create a Loving Relationship That Lasts* (Berkeley, CA: Parallax Press, 2011), 81.

47   The Karmapa, Ogyen Trinley Dorje, *The Heart is Noble: Changing the World from the Inside Out* (Boston, MA: Shambhala Publications, 2013), 26.

48   Chögyam Trungpa Rinpoche, *Training the Mind and Cultivating Loving-Kindness* (Boston, MA: Shambhala Publications, 1993), 29.

49   Pema Chödrön, "How Lojong Awakens Your Heart," *Lion's Roar*, November 22, 2017, https://www.lionsroar.com/dont-give-up/.

50   Sharon Salzberg, "Maintaining Hope in Hard Times," *Ten Percent Happier*, October 16, 2019, https://www.tenpercent.com/meditationweeklyblog/ maintaining-hope-in-hard-times.

51   Traleg Kyabgon, *The Practice of Lojong: Cultivating Compassion Through Training the Mind* (Boston, MA: Shambhala Publications, 2007), 97.

52   Chögyam Trungpa Rinpoche, "Timely Rain," in *Timely Rain: Selected Poetry of Chögyam Trungpa* (Boston, MA: Shambhala Publications, 1998), 35.

53   At this point in my life, I find this particular barb to be more complimentary than I used to. My mother is really nice; you should meet her if you can.

54   Sharon Salzberg, *Real Happiness: The Power of Meditation* (New York, NY: Workman Publishing Company, 2010), 104.

55 Chögyam Trungpa Rinpoche, *Work, Sex, Money* (Boston, MA: Shambhala Publications, 2011), 195.

56 Chögyam Trungpa Rinpoche, *Work, Sex, Money* (Boston, MA: Shambhala Publications, 2011), 172.

57 David Chadwick (ed.), *Zen is Right Here* (Boston, MA: Shambhala Publications, 2001), 39.

58 Baltasar Gracián, *The Art of World Wisdom* (Boston, MA: Shambhala Publications, 1993), 60.

59 Millicent Fenwick, *Vogue's Book of Etiquette* (New York: Simon and Schuster, 1948), 16.

60 Philip Gollanes, *New York Times*, December 8th, 2016.

61 Thich Nhat Hanh, *How to Love* (Parallax Press, Berkeley, 2015), p. 67.

62 John Lewis, interview by Krista Tippett, *On Being with Krista Tippett*, March 28, 2013, https://onbeing.org/programs/john-lewis-love-in-action-jan2017/.

63 Baltasar Gracián, *The Art of World Wisdom* (Boston, MA: Shambhala Publications, 1993), 185.

64 John Bridges, *How to Be a Gentleman* (Nashville, TN: Thomas Nelson, 1998), 106.

65 Philip Gollanes, *New York Times*, March 9th, 2017.

66 Chögyam Trungpa Rinpoche, *Shambhala: Sacred Path of the Warrior* (Boston, MA: Shambhala Publications, 2007), 15.

67 Shantideva, *The Way of the Bodhisattva* (Boston, MA: Shambhala Publications, 2012), 118.

68 John Bridges, *How to Be a Gentleman* (Nashville, TN: Thomas Nelson, 1998), 38.

69 Graham Greene, *May We Borrow Your Husband?* (London: The Bodley Head, 1967).

70 The Karmapa, Ogyen Trinley Dorje, *The Heart is Noble: Changing the World from the Inside Out* (Boston, MA: Shambhala Publications, 2013), 25–26.

71 Thich Nhat Hanh, *How to Fight* (Berkeley, CA: Parallax Press, 2017), 8.

72 Thich Nhat Hanh, *How to Fight* (Berkeley, CA: Parallax Press, 2017), 103.

73 Millicent Fenwick, *Vogue's Book of Etiquette* (New York: Simon and Schuster, 1948), 235.

74 Pema Chödrön, "Smile at Fear: Pema Chödrön on Bravery, Open Heart & Basic Goodness," *Lion's Roar*, October 31, 2018, https://www.lionsroar.com/smile-at-fear-pema-chodrons-teachings-on-bravery-open-heart-basic-goodness/.

Acknowledgments

I am always moved when anyone reads my books. This is my seventh, and the awe of you holding this thing in your hand and engaging in it as if we were sitting across a dining room table chatting is still so, so moving to me. You are the best. Thank you.

This book would not have come to fruition if not for certain lovely people. Thank you to my agent, Stephanie Tade, who believed in it and saw what it would become before I did, as well as to Alice Peck, my wonderful editor who was so thoughtful in her approach to this book. Alice challenged me not just to make this a better book but to aim to become a better writer. I hope I haven't let you down. Diedre Hammons took her keen eyes and polished this thing beyond belief. Jess Morphew has championed my work in myriad ways over the years and did the exquisite work on the cover and interior. I am lucky to have my book guided by such wise and insightful women.

My love and gratitude goes out to the friends who bought me drinks, told me stories and recommended resources for this book such as Jeff Grow, Juan Carlos Castro, Ericka Phillips, Laura Sinkman, Dave Perrin, Marina Acosta, Tom Krieglstein, Rodney Solomon, Matt Bonaccorso, Brett Eggleston, David Delcourt and Dev Aujla. My mother, Beth Rinzler, has always been there for me in the ways that matter the most and for that I am deeply grateful.

I am lucky to have colleagues, mentors and teachers from many Buddhist traditions. I thank them and hope to honor them with my work: Susan Piver, Lama Rod Owens, Charlie Morley, Sharon Salzberg, Frank Ryan, Kilung Rinpoche and Thich Nhat Hanh to name but a few cherished individuals.

Finally, I am lost if not for Adreanna Limbach, my wife. She is so unbelievably kind, which includes kindly pointing out my blindspots, and that has shaped this book tremendously. For this brief moment, I need to say out loud that any of the work I do that benefits others is only possible because of the love of this woman. Your grace, gentleness, and discernment guide me in ways you may not always know. I love you, and thank you for agreeing to spend your life with me.

Thank you all so much for breathing life into this book. May it help many people.

About the Author

Lodro Rinzler is the author of seven meditation books including *The Buddha Walks into a Bar* and *Love Hurts: Buddhist Advice for the Heartbroken*. His books *Walk Like a Buddha* and *The Buddha Walks into the Office* both have received Independent Publisher Book Awards. He has taught meditation for twenty years in the Tibetan Buddhist tradition and travels frequently for his books, having spoken across the world at conferences, universities, and businesses as diverse as Google, Harvard University and the White House. He lives in upstate New York with his wife Adreanna and a swarm of furry beings and personally responds to every note a reader sends him via lodrorinzler.com.

Also by Lodro

Made in the USA
Las Vegas, NV
29 September 2022

56159909R00142